HOW TO PASS

In full COLOUR

KV-578-881

STANDARD GRADE

BUSINESS MANAGEMENT

Peter Hagan

HODDER
GIBSON
PART OF HACHETTE UK

The Publishers would like to thank the following for permission to reproduce copyright material:

Photo credits

Fig 2.1 © DC Graphic Design Limited; Fig 2.4 © Bob Fleumer/zefa/Corbis; Fig 2.5 Ken McKay / Rex Features; Fig 3.2 Andisheh Eslamboli / Rex Features; Fig 5.1(right) © J Sainsbury plc; Fig 5.4(left) With kind permission by Virgin Media; Fig 5.4 (right) With kind permission by Nike; Fig 7.2 © Friedrich Stark / Alamy; Fig 7.3 Sipa Press / Rex Features; Fig 7.4 © Megapress / Alamy; Fig 8.2 reproduced with permission of s1; Fig 8.3 Rex Features; Fig 9.2 © Steve Chenn/Corbis; Fig 10.1 and 10.2 reproduced by kind permission of the Scottish Qualifications Authority.

All other photos © Hodder Gibson.

Acknowledgements

The course aims from the Standard Grade Business Management Arrangements document and questions from past exam papers are reproduced with permission of the Scottish Qualifications Authority.

Every effort has been made to trace all copyright holders, but if any have been inadvertently overlooked the Publishers will be pleased to make the necessary arrangements at the first opportunity.

Although every effort has been made to ensure that website addresses are correct at time of going to press, Hodder Gibson cannot be held responsible for the content of any website mentioned in this book. It is sometimes possible to find a relocated web page by typing in the address of the home page for a website in the URL window of your browser.

Hachette's policy is to use papers that are natural, renewable and recyclable products and made from wood grown in sustainable forests. The logging and manufacturing processes are expected to conform to the environmental regulations of the country of origin.

Orders: please contact Bookpoint Ltd, 130 Milton Park, Abingdon, Oxon OX14 4SB. Telephone: (44) 01235 827720. Fax: (44) 01235 400454. Lines are open 9.00–5.00, Monday to Saturday, with a 24-hour message answering service. Visit our website at www.hoddereducation.co.uk. Hodder Gibson can be contacted direct on: Tel: 0141 848 1609; Fax: 0141 889 6315; email: hoddergibson@hodder.co.uk

© Peter Hagan 2009
First published in 2009 by
Hodder Gibson, an imprint of Hodder Education,
Part of Hachette UK,
2a Christie Street
Paisley PA1 1NB

Impression number   5 4 3 2 1
Year   2012 2011 2010 2009

Cover photo Purestock/Ingram Publishing/Getty Images
Illustrations by DC Graphic Design Limited, Swanley Village, Kent
Typeset in Frutiger Light 10.5 by DC Graphic Design Limited, Swanley Village, Kent
Printed in Italy

A catalogue record for this title is available from the British Library

ISBN-13: 978 0340 973 875

CONTENTS

PREPARING FOR THE EXAM

Welcome to this Revision Book!

This book is designed to help you prepare for the examination at the end of the Standard Grade Business Management course and gain as high a grade as you possibly can. It is not a textbook, but a guide to how to pass at the Levels you are entered for.

The book is arranged around the topics you have covered or will cover in your course. It does not follow the Units that you may have studied in school, but has grouped together the parts of each topic because it is often easier to study a whole topic, like marketing, as one, rather than in bits and pieces in the Units.

Your course notes may be in order of Units so I have included the Areas of Study from the Scottish Qualifications Authority (SQA) Arrangements in the Appendix at the back of this book to help you refer to your own notes while using this book.

There are four areas of study in the Standard Grade Business Management course:

1   What is business?
2   How do businesses develop and perform?
3   What resources do businesses use?
4   How are businesses managed?

The Exam

Like most Standard Grade subjects, Business Management can be sat at three different Levels – Foundation, General, and Credit. On the day of the exam you will sit either both the Foundation and General Levels, or both the General and Credit Levels.

By then you will have spent almost two years studying the course, so you should have lots to write about.

The exams are designed to allow you to show how much you have learned and understand about Business Management, and to apply it to a range of different scenarios.

Sitting SQA exams for the first time can be quite a scary prospect for most pupils. The first thing I have to tell you is not to worry, or, rather, not to worry too much – you still have to study for them.

Exams can be quite stressful but there are things you can do to help take off some of the pressure *and* also get better exam grades.

This book will help you do this, and make you as confident as you possibly can be that you will get the grade that your knowledge deserves in the exam.

We will look at:

◆ exam technique – how to get full marks and avoid losing marks

◆ problem questions in the exam

◆ the areas of study and what is included in them

◆ exam-type revision questions for each of the areas of study

◆ the 'Business@Work' project.

Summary

The course aims are specified by the SQA. They are to:

◆ develop knowledge and understanding of the nature and importance of business activity

◆ develop knowledge and understanding of the process of business formation and development

◆ develop knowledge and understanding of how businesses acquire and manage resources

◆ develop understanding of the different ways in which individuals contribute to business activity

◆ develop awareness of the internal structures of organisations and how these may influence activities

◆ develop skills in decision making

◆ develop ability to use business software as an aid to management decision making

◆ develop awareness of the importance of team work

◆ provide a foundation for progression to Intermediate or Higher courses in Business Management and other related courses

◆ provide a foundation for future education and training in Business Management or related subjects.

Foundation Level

The Foundation paper lasts for one hour and normally has the highest number of questions of all the papers. The answers expected here are what we call short response answers. This means that many of the questions can be answered with one or two words or a short sentence.

Some candidates find this paper quite difficult because they are looking for something harder in the question. If you are sitting foundation level make sure you get plenty of practice using past papers so you get used to the style of questions asked.

You can download copies of the most recent past papers from the SQA website for free (www.sqa.org.uk). You can also get copies of the marking schemes or solutions on the website to check your answers.

General Level

The General paper lasts for one hour and fifteen minutes. Here the answers are expected to have more development than at Foundation level. There are only a few questions where one-word answers are expected so it is good practice to try to answer each question in a sentence.

It is also expected that you will be able to justify many of the answers you give. This appears to be a problem area for many candidates because they do not really understand what justification means.

We will look at this problem in more detail a little later on when we look at questions that ask you to suggest and justify – the justification is your explanation as to why you think your suggestion is a good one.

Again, you can download recent past papers and marking schemes from the SQA website. Just remember that the marking schemes or solutions are guides to those marking the papers and could include one-word answers where you, on the other hand, would be expected to write more.

Both the Foundation and General Level papers have spaces for you to write your answers, so this will give you some indication of how long your answer should be.

Credit Level

The Credit paper lasts for one and a half hours and has five main questions. However, each question is split into a number of parts which you have to respond to. This is obviously the most difficult paper of the three but the questions are straightforward and easy to understand.

The hard part is knowing all the right answers and explaining yourself properly. There are no spaces for answers in the question paper, which means you can write as much as you like. There is no negative marking so you don't need to worry about losing marks for an incorrect part of your answer. Write as much as you can – you will get marks for all of the correct answers you give.

The Elements in the Exam

Each paper (Foundation/General/Credit) is split into two elements. Together these parts make up two thirds of your grade. The other third is for the Practical Abilities Project, which we will look at later in the book. The two elements in the exam are **Knowledge and Understanding (KU)** and **Decision Making (DM)**.

Knowledge and Understanding

Key Points

The course should develop knowledge and understanding of:

◆ concepts central to the operation of different types of business enterprise, including voluntary organisations

◆ similarities and differences between different enterprises

◆ how business enterprise operates in contemporary society

◆ the relationship between business activity and the social and economic environment within which it takes place

◆ the role that management plays in the effectiveness of business.

Knowledge and Understanding will test you on the theory that you have learned in the course and will ask questions such as:

'Identify the elements of the marketing mix.'

It concentrates on the concepts that you have learned in the course.

Decision Making

> ### Key Points
>
> The course should develop decision-making skills used in business through:
> - gathering, processing and evaluating information
> - the correct use of information
> - making valid judgements and conclusions based on information collected.

Decision Making will ask you to apply what you have learned to different situations such as:

'Suggest and justify two methods of extending the life cycle of AB plc's product.'

Decision Making allows you to make judgements and draw conclusions, so unlike Knowledge and Understanding it is not about simply learning facts, but about how to use that knowledge.

With Knowledge and Understanding there is usually only one correct answer (although you may need to write more than one thing), whereas with Decision Making there are often a range of answers you can pick from. You will have the opportunity to develop your answer by explaining what you have written.

The total number of marks allocated for each element is roughly the same.

The Exam

You actually started preparing for the exam at the beginning of the course – but here we will look at ways of getting your brain into gear so it is as sharp as possible on the exam day itself.

Your brain is like a muscle: you have to exercise it to keep it in shape.

You should spend 10–15 minutes every evening learning something. The trick is to make it easy to learn.

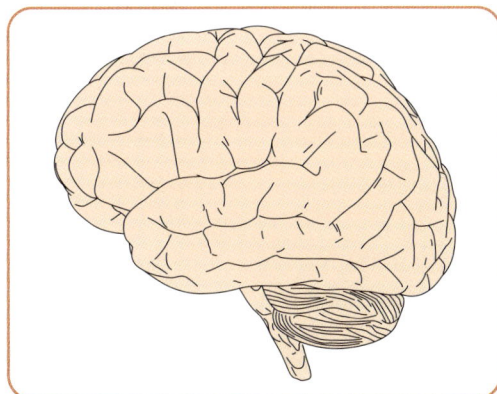

Figure 1.1 Exercise your brain!

Hints and Tips

In the exam many pupils have trouble remembering the external factors for a business's environment. Look at the following list:

Political

Economic

Socio-cultural

Technological

Environmental

Competitive

It is easy to remember the word PESTEC but it is a bit harder to remember what the letters stand for. Spend a couple of minutes memorising them, then write them down.

Your brain has now filed this information for you to use when you need it. Unfortunately you probably won't get many marks in the exam for simply remembering a list of the external factors so we have to give your brain some more exercise.

The list of examples below has a word or phrase in each highlighted for you to remember.

Political	The government may bring in **new laws**.
Economic	The economy can move between **growth and recession**.
Socio-cultural	Consumers' **tastes can change**.
Technological	**New** technology can be introduced that the business needs to use.
Environmental	Businesses need to reduce their **'carbon footprint'**.
Competitive	Competitors can **reduce their prices**.

Now try to memorise the examples and then write them out a couple of times from memory.

Congratulations – you now know what the external factors are and can give examples of them.

Hints and *Tips continued* ➢

Hints and Tips continued

You should try this approach with other areas where you think you may have a problem – keep exercising your brain!

Of course there is still a problem. Your brain has its own filing system – it keeps things in different places from where you would probably want. You have to train your brain to remember things together.

The best way to do this is to organise the information on paper. So sort out your folders – make sure all those loose pieces of paper are put into the right section (use dividers) and number your folders. Doing this will allow your brain to organise all your knowledge of business management together.

The following websites will be helpful in your studies:

www.businessstudiesonline.co.uk (includes games to help you learn)

www.bbc.co.uk/schools/gcsebitesize (select Business Studies)

www.sqa.org.uk (select 'services for centres' and then Business Management)

www.sportstore.org.uk (register and run your own sports store)

www.bbc.co.uk/workinglunch (click on the link for lunch lessons – there are short videos with good case studies to help you understand some of the topics you cover)

www.bized.co.uk (useful glossary of key terms and theory for getting answers quickly when doing your Practical Abilities Project – just use the search facility)

EXAM TECHNIQUE

Getting Full Marks for Your Answers

Hints and Tips

There are some things you can do to make sure you get full marks for your answer.

Don't use one-word answers unless you are asked – always put your answer in a sentence. You will *never* be asked for one-word answers at Credit Level!

Use the right business terms. Words such as easier or quicker don't usually attract marks. You need to say why it is easier or quicker. Below is a list of common words or phrases found in pupils' answers that should *not* be used on their own in an answer:

Quicker
Easier
Saves time
Saves money
Internet
Make money
Sack workers

Example

'Suggest and justify an action a business could take when they find they are no longer profitable.'   (2 DM)

You answer should be:

They could make some staff redundant. By reducing the number of staff they could reduce the level of expenses.   (2 marks)

Your answer should not be:

Sack workers to save money.   (0 marks)

Command words

These are the words used in the exam questions that tell you what you are supposed to do.

The following are examples of command words used in the exam.

Command word	Definition
Give	List some of the key points
Describe	Give a full account of the word, phrase etc.
Identify/name	Name the main point or points
Name	Identify or make a list
Suggest	State a possible reason or course of action (no development required)
Justify	Give reasons to support suggestions, conclusions
Explain (usually a term)	Show that you understand the point being asked by giving details about it

Let's look at some examples of how to respond to the command words correctly. The following question comes from the 2006 Credit Paper about the fashion store Zara.

Example

'Suggest and describe 2 ways in which Zara can **gather information** to give customers fashions they want.'   (4 DM)

You should firstly *suggest* a way that Zara can gather information and then *describe* what you mean.

Answer
They could use observation. (This is the suggestion and earns you 1 mark.)

By watching customers in stores and their reaction to products. (This is the justification and earns you 1 mark).

They could look at Internet websites. (Suggestion = 1 mark)

Fashion websites may show what customers want now and in the future. (Justification = 1 mark).

This answer would earn all 4 marks.

The answers are all sentences.

Example *continued* ➢

Example *continued*

The answer uses the term 'Internet websites' rather than just 'Internet', which would probably not get a mark on its own.

The answer also refers to the stimulus material about the fashion store. You should always try to answer in the context of the question.

Decision making

One change in the exam in recent years is that it is now more difficult to get marks for the Decision-making element in the exam. If, for example, you are asked to justify your answers then you need to give different justifications for those answers in order to get full marks.

Example

'Suggest and justify **2** ways in which Greggs [bakery] could grow in size. Give **2 different** justifications.' (2 DM)

For your suggestions you could write:

Open more stores (1 mark) and

Take over another bakery business (1 mark).

However, if you gave the same justification for both you would only get one justification mark.

It would increase the number of customers (1 mark).

To get full marks you could write that opening more stores would allow the business to target new markets, and that taking over another bakery business would increase market share.

Of course, it is always better to use the correct terms when answering questions. Opening new stores is *Internal Growth*, and taking over another bakery business would be *Horizontal Integration*.

Developing your answers

Another recent change in the exam is what you should write for marketing questions in order to get full marks. An example used by the examiners recently was on methods of advertising. If, for example, you had suggested television advertising as a method of promotion for a business, they would not accept very basic answers such as:

Because a lot of people watch television.

They are now looking for more developed answers such as:

They could use television advertising as they can use a mixture of sound, images, colour and voice-over to create a strong impression of their product.

Or

They can use TV advertising as they can target certain market segments by advertising during particular programmes that appeal to those segments, e.g. teenagers during Hollyoaks.

Answering in context

You should always try to answer each question in context. What does this mean?

Each question in the exam is based on a business. The introduction to the question (called the stem or stimulus material) tells you a little about the business. This is done to help you answer the questions and guide you to give the sort of answer the examiners are looking for.

Example

Amazon.com is one of the biggest 'e-commerce' businesses in the world. Amazon.com sells a wide variety of goods and services on-line. Amazon's UK distribution centre is a large warehouse for storing stock. However, you won't see space-age robots picking goods off shelves. Labour-intensive processing is used, with hands stuffing books into pigeon holes, stacking CDs onto shelves and moving electrical appliances around the warehouse floor.

A huge banner above the workers' heads reads 'Safety protects people. Quality protects customers.'

(Adapted from 'the Internet' Magazine, September 2003)

'Describe the **features of a suitable stock storage area** for Amazon.' (3 KU)

Example continued ➤

Example *continued*

The question being about Amazon, one of the biggest e-commerce businesses in the world, would allow you to assume that they have a huge number of customers and handle a huge number of stock items.

There are lots of small e-commerce businesses who can operate very well by using a back bedroom as a suitable storage area for their stock, as long as it is secure. If the question was simply about any e-commerce business then the back bedroom would be an acceptable answer.

However, the question is about Amazon and so this would not be acceptable. The answers you give must be about a very large business.

Answer
They would need a large amount of space so that all stock can be stored and moved easily.

They would need to have a very good security system to ensure no stock is stolen.

They would need an efficient stock control system so that they know what they have and where it is.

Problem Questions

There are a number of areas of the course where candidates have not performed very well in recent years. We will take a look at some of the main problem topics and see if your knowledge would get you full marks in an exam.

'I don't like finance!'

Finance seems to be a difficult area for some pupils. Many of them have had 'bad' experiences with their maths lessons and have a fear of numbers. If this sounds like you, then please don't be afraid of finance – it isn't maths.

Many of the answers you are asked for are theory only, and you are not often asked to do calculations except for ratios. Although Finance is a very important part of the course, it is relatively small and not too difficult to understand – honest!

Figure 2.1 Finance is a vital part of business management

The best way to deal with finance is to do as many questions as you can, over and over again if necessary. Once you start to remember things about this area of the course, the better you will understand it.

Ratios

You only have to remember five ratios and their formulae, and also what can happen to improve them or make them worse. Try memorising each of their names and then the formula used to calculate them.

Summary

A quick summary of ratios:

1   Gross Profit as a Percentage of Sales – this shows the % profit a firm has made on buying and selling stock.

(Gross Profit ÷ Net Sales) × 100

2   Net Profit as a Percentage of Sales – this shows the % overall profit made by the business.

(Net Profit ÷ Net Sales) × 100

3   Rate of Stock Turnover – this shows how quickly the business buys and sells stock.

Cost of Goods Sold ÷ Average Stock (Opening + Closing Stock ÷ 2)

4   Return on Capital Employed (ROCE) – this shows the % of profit earned for every £1 of capital invested.

(Net Profit ÷ Capital at Start) × 100

5   Working Capital – this shows the ability of the business to pay its current debts.

Current Assets ÷ Current Liabilities

Ratio	Possible reasons for changes
Gross Profit %	Change in selling price Change in the cost of purchases Stock losses, e.g. theft, damage, waste
Net Profit %	All of the above, plus Changes in expenses
Rate of Stock Turnover	Changes in sales levels Changes in the level of stock held
Return on Capital Employed	Changes in the level of Net Profit
Working Capital	Changes in any of the current assets (cash, bank, stock, debtors, etc.), or Changes in the level of current liabilities (creditors, bank overdraft, etc.)

Let us look at some past paper questions on ratios.

Example

Anita Sadiq started her mobile hairdressing service a year ago. She has now prepared her final accounts for the first year and is quite pleased with the results.

Here is Anita's Trading, Profit and Loss Account:

Hair at Home **Trading, Profit and Loss Account** **for the period ending 31 March 2006**		
	£	£
Sales		35,000
Less: Cost of Sales		
Opening Stock	6,200	
Add: Purchases	12,300	
	18,500	
Less: Closing Stock	4,200	
		14,300
GROSS PROFIT		20,700
Less: Expenses		
Telephone Calls	1,200	
Petrol	1,600	
Advertising	1,000	
Miscellaneous	500	
		4,300
NET PROFIT		16,400

(a) (i) Identify **2 profitability ratios** that Anita could use to analyse her Trading, Profit and Loss Account. (2 KU)

(ii) Using the figures from Anita's Trading, Profit and Loss Account, **calculate one of the ratios** you have identified above. (3 DM)

In this question we are told that Anita Sadiq is a mobile hairdresser and we are shown her Trading, Profit and Loss Account for her first year.

Question (a) (i) asks you to identify two profitability ratios.

Example continued ➤

Example *continued*

The two profitability ratios that you are taught in the Standard Grade Business Management course are:

Gross Profit (as a percentage of sales)

and

Net Profit (as a percentage of sales).

In this question you are asked only to identify them, so you do not need to show the formulae for them yet.

Question (a) (ii) then asks you to calculate one of the ratios above. We will do both.

For the Gross Profit ratio we only need 2 figures – the Gross Profit figure, which is £20,700, and the Sales figure, which is £35,000.

All we need to do is divide £20,700 by £35,000 and multiply this by 100. You can use your calculator to do this.

It is worth reminding you at this stage to take a calculator with you into the exam. Don't panic if you forget, the invigilator should be able to give you one.

$$\frac{20{,}700}{35{,}000} \times 100$$

= 59%

Remember this is a percentage ratio, so always put the percentage sign after your answer to get full marks.

The Net Profit Ratio is very similar to the Gross Profit. You just replace Gross Profit with Net Profit.

The Net Profit figure is £16,400, so the calculation would be:

$$\frac{16{,}400}{35{,}000} \times 100$$

= 47%

Now let us look at an example of a question from a General paper.

Example

Harry McKie owns an Internet café called Flexinet that has been open for a year. He has prepared the following financial information and is concerned because the figures are not as he expected when he prepared his business plan.

Flexinet Internet Café Finance Information January–February 2005		
	January	February
Gross Profit % Ratio	42%	38%
Net Profit % Ratio	20%	19%
Cash Flow Balance	£850	(£250)

(a) Suggest **one** possible reason why the Gross Profit % Ratio for Flexinet has fallen. (1 DM)

(b) What is the formula for the Net Profit % Ratio? (2 KU)

Here we are given the Gross Profit and Net Profit Ratios for the months of January and February for the Flexinet Internet Café.

Question (a) asks you to suggest one possible reason why the Gross Profit % for Flexinet has fallen.

Gross Profit is calculated by subtracting the Cost of Sales from the Sales figure.

	£
Sales	30,000
Cost of Sales	10,000
Gross Profit	20,000

The Sales figure is based on the number sold and the selling price, and the Cost of Sales is based on how much it cost the business to buy the things that it sold. Therefore the two most likely causes of changing the Gross Profit Ratio are:

A change in the selling price

A change in the purchase price.

Example continued ➤

> ### *Example* *continued*
>
> So for the Gross Profit Ratio to fall, either the selling price has fallen or the Cost of Purchases has increased. It could also be an indication that stock is being wasted in some way, such as going out of date, being stolen, etc.
>
> Your answer to Question (a) could include:
>
> ◆ *the selling price being lowered*
> ◆ *the Cost of Purchases increasing*
> ◆ *poor stock control.*
>
> Question (b) asks you for the formula for the Net Profit % Ratio.
>
> The answer is simply:
>
> *Net Profit ÷ Sales × 100*

Cash Budgets

Drawing up budgets makes very good business sense and makes sure that your business survives. Remember most businesses fail because they do not have enough money to pay their bills when they are due to be paid, rather than because they are not making a profit.

Imagine an imitation Christmas tree manufacturer. They may spend all year making trees and having to pay their workers, electricity bills, phone bills, bills for their raw materials, etc., but they only get paid for what they produce around Christmas time!

They always have to be very careful to make sure that they have cash to pay these expenses even when no money is coming into the business from sales.

At the end of the year when they are paid, the business might have made a good profit, but if they didn't pay their bills during the year then the workers would leave, their phone and electricity would be cut off, and they would have no supplies. This is why Cash Budgets are so important.

So what do you look out for in a question?

Well firstly, look for any negative closing balances. This would mean the business would run out of cash that month and would be unable to pay its bills unless it arranges a bank overdraft or brings in cash from somewhere else.

Secondly, look at the money coming in from sales. Is it falling? If it is then you would have to worry about running out of cash in the future, and possibly look at reducing some of your costs.

Lastly, look at the money going out of the business. Are any of the costs rising? If they are it could mean that your expenses are getting out of control and you should look at ways of reducing them. This could mean making some staff redundant, looking for new suppliers, or cutting back on some expenses.

Let's look at a recent example of a Credit Level budget question.

Example

Fredo Franchi's fast food business has been running for one year now and he has plans to expand by opening another shop. His brother Carlo is considering joining him in partnership and wants to look at the business finances. Fredo has prepared a Cash Budget for him to look at before making a decision.

CASH BUDGET – FRANCHI FAST FOODS

JUNE–AUGUST 2007

	June	July	August
Opening Balance	£500	£2,300	–£1,000
Cash In			
Sales	£27,500	£30,000	£33,000
	£28,000	£32,300	£32,000
Cash Out			
Purchases	£10,600	£15,000	£13,000
Wages	£9,600	£10,500	£11,500
Expenses	£5,500	£7,800	£9,800
	£25,700	£33,300	£34,300
Closing Balance	£2,300	–£1,000	–£2,300

(a) Explain the **purpose** of preparing a Cash Budget. (2 KU)

Example continued ➤

Example *continued*

(b) (i) Give **3** reasons why Carlo might be concerned about the cashflow situation.

(3 DM)

(ii) Suggest **appropriate action** that can be taken to improve the **3** problems you have identified above.

(3 DM)

Question (b) (i) asks you to give 3 reasons why Carlo might be concerned about the cashflow situation.

Closing balances

◆ The first obvious problem is that in both July and August there were negative closing balances.

◆ This would mean that Fredo would not have the money to pay for purchases, wages, and expenses.

◆ More importantly, each month the closing balance shows a trend that Fredo has more cash going out of the business than coming in.

Looking at each of the other lines of information in turn we should be able to identify other concerns that Carlo might have.

Sales

◆ The sales figure is increasing each month, which is good and nothing to worry about.

Purchases

◆ The purchases figure is also growing and you would expect him to be buying more food as his sales are growing.

◆ However, there seems to have been a big increase in July to £15,000.

◆ This is not matched by as big an increase in sales and if this increase was spent on food supplies then either he has reduced his prices to sell more, or there is a lot of food being wasted.

◆ The other possibility is that he has purchased a new piece of equipment that he possibly could not afford at this time, but we are not given enough information to know this.

Example continued ➢

Example *continued*

Wages

◆ Wages are also rising and this should be a concern to Carlo as it is adding to the problems with the closing balances.

◆ However, he may need more staff to cope with the increased sales.

Expenses

◆ Expenses are also increasing.

◆ Carlo should be concerned because this is adding to the cash going out during the month.

◆ Fredo may be increasing advertising in order to increase sales, but we are not told this.

You will notice that all we have discussed so far is the concerns – not what could be done about them. This is because you are asked about that in the second part of question (b).

You are asked to suggest appropriate action that can be taken to improve the 3 problems identified.

Closing balances

◆ If this is a short term problem then Fredo could approach his bank about arranging an overdraft.

◆ Or he could invest some of his own money into the business.

◆ Fredo could also try to raise more cash by increasing his prices, or by trying to sell more.

Purchases

◆ Fredo could look for cheaper suppliers.

◆ He could ask for bigger discounts from his suppliers.

◆ He could ask for longer to pay so that he can sell the food before he pays for it.

Wages

◆ Fredo could cut back on his workers' hours in order to reduce the amount going out on wages.

◆ Or he could make one of them redundant.

Expenses

Fredo could reduce some expenses such as telephone, advertising, etc.

Let's look at a General Level example.

Example

Cash Budget of Francisco Rodrigo For 3 months January–March 2006			
	January (£)	February (£)	March (£)
Opening Balance	500	2,400	5,000
Cash In			
Sales	13,000	14,700	15,500
	13,500	**17,100**	**20,500**
Cash Out			
Purchases	9,000	10,000	12,000
Wages	700	700	700
Rent	800	800	800
Heating and Lighting	600	600	600
Purchase of Machine	0	0	8,000
	11,100	**12,100**	**22,100**
Closing Balance	2,400	5,000	(1,600)

(a) (i) Which month had the **lowest sales**? (1 DM)

(ii) Which month had the **highest total payments**? (1 DM)

(b) Explain what has happened to the closing balance in March. (1 DM)

(c) Suggest **2 changes** which could have been made to improve the closing balance in March. (2 DM)

Here we are shown the cash budget of Francisco Rodrigo for the months of January, February and March.

General questions are more straightforward.

Question (a) (i) asks which month has the lowest sales figures.

Looking along the line at the sales figures we can see that January has the lowest sales figure with £13,000. February has £14,700 and March £15,500.

Question (a) (ii) asks which month had the highest total payments.

Looking along the line we can see that January has £11,100, February £12,100 and March £22,100. So the answer is March.

Example continued ➢

Example *continued*

Question (b) asks you to explain what has happened to the closing balance in March.

The figure of £1,600 is in brackets, which tells us that it is a negative figure. This means that there is more money going out of the business than is due to come in that month, even after adding on the opening balance.

Looking at the cash out for that month we can see that there has been a large expense in the form of a machine purchased for £8,000.

Question (c) then asks you to suggest 2 changes which could have been made to improve the closing balance in March.

There are a number of possible solutions to this. Probably the most obvious was not to buy the machine with cash. If it was necessary to have it then it could have been leased, or bought on credit with a bank loan, or Francisco could have put more money into the business to buy the machine.

Other possible solutions could be:

◆ increase revenue from sales
◆ reduce spending on purchases – find cheaper supplier
◆ reduce staff to reduce wages/reduce number of hours staff work
◆ find cheaper premises
◆ conserve energy
◆ advertise or have promotions to try and sell more
◆ reduce rent/expenses/costs.

Fixed and Variable Costs

Fixed Costs stay the same from month to month, no matter how much you produce. You would still have to pay them even if you produced nothing. Good examples would be things like rent, rates, insurance and loan repayments.

Variable Costs increase with the amount you produce, so the more you make, the more you have to pay. The obvious example here would be the cost of raw materials but you may also have to pay more for things like delivery, packaging and wages.

Let us have a look at a past paper question on Fixed and Variable Costs.

Example

Study the information below and then answer the questions that follow.

Malik and Co Ltd manufactures toy cars. Below is a table showing its Fixed Costs and Variable Costs of production.

COSTS OF PRODUCTION		
Output	Fixed Costs	Variable Costs
1,000	10,000	30,000
2,000	10,000	45,000
3,000	10,000	60,000
4,000	10,000	70,000

(a) Explain the terms:

    (i) Fixed Costs

    (ii) Variable Costs   (2 KU)

(b) Give an example for Malik and Co Ltd of:

    (i) A Fixed Cost

    (ii) A Variable Cost   (2 DM)

Here you are shown the Fixed and Variable Costs at various levels of output, but the question does not ask you to use these figures.

Question (a) asks you to explain the terms Fixed Costs and Variable Costs.

Your answer should be:

Fixed Costs are costs that do not change or vary with the level of production/output.

Variable Costs change as production/output changes.

This means that Variable Costs will increase if production increases, and decrease if production decreases.

Example *continued* ➤

Example *continued*

Question (b) asks you to give an example of a Fixed Cost and an example of a Variable Cost.

Your answer could include:

Fixed Cost – rent, rates, insurance, salaries

Variable Cost – materials, labour, electricity.

Channels of distribution

Many pupils get confused between 'channels of distribution' and 'methods of distribution' (transportation).

Channels of distribution are about whether you sell directly to your customer or whether you use wholesalers, retailers or agents. The diagram below shows the main channels of distribution available to businesses.

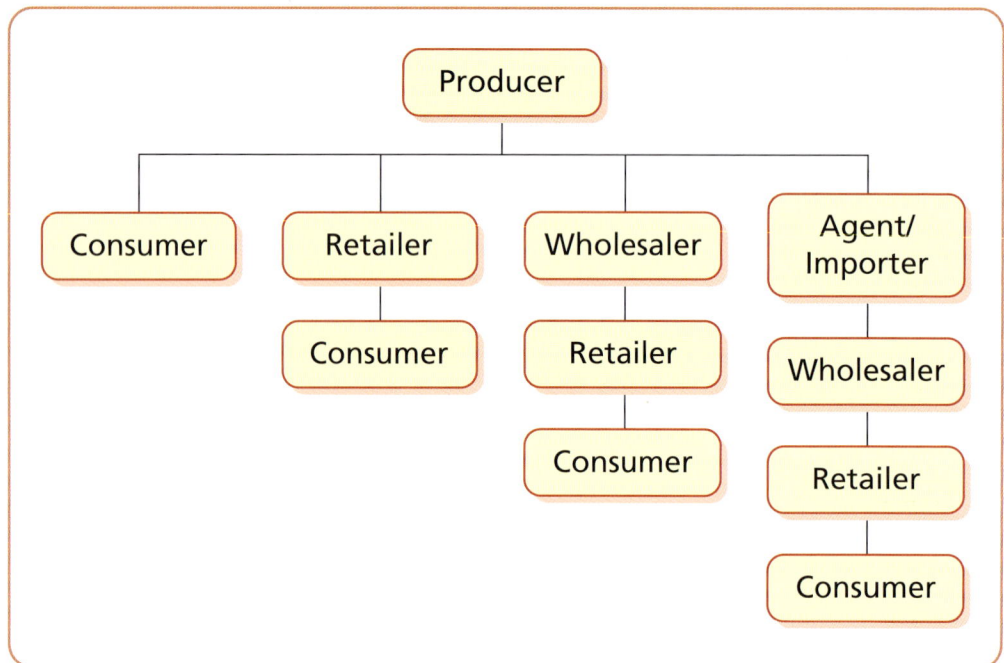

```
                         Producer
        ┌───────────────┬───────────────┬───────────────┐
     Consumer       Retailer        Wholesaler      Agent/Importer
                        │               │               │
                     Consumer        Retailer        Wholesaler
                                        │               │
                                     Consumer         Retailer
                                                        │
                                                     Consumer
```

Figure 2.2 The channels of distribution

Some businesses prefer to sell directly to their customers because they can keep full control of marketing and don't have to share their profits.

The main benefits of selling indirectly are that:

◆ wholesalers will take large amounts of stock, meaning you won't have to store it

◆ wholesalers may finish off the packaging and pricing

◆ wholesalers will be motivated to get the customers for your product

◆ retailers/shops will display your goods for sale to the public and provide information, finance packages for the customers, and some after sales services.

Pricing strategies

The term 'pricing strategies' can often cause problems for pupils.

Put simply, if you are asked what pricing strategies a business can use, then all you are being asked is how can the price of the product be used or changed to help the product sell. Another way of putting the question is how will raising or lowering the price help sell the product?

The main pricing strategies are:

Long term	
Low price	Charge a lower price than your competitors where lower prices will result in much higher sales.
Market price	Setting prices broadly in line with those of competitors.
High price	Where the business offers high quality, premium goods and services where image is important.
Short term	
Skimming	This involves charging a high price at first, usually for a new product where there is little competition. Eventually the price may be lowered.
Penetration pricing (low price)	This is usually used in order to introduce a product to an established market and allows the business to achieve sales and gain market share very quickly.
Destroyer pricing	Setting a price below those of competitors, but this time at an artificially low price in order to destroy the competition.
Promotional pricing	This is used to boost sales in the short term by lowering the price of the product. It can also be used to create interest in a new product.
Demand-orientated pricing	Where price varies along with the demand for the product. High demand equals high price; low demand equals low price.

Computerised stock control system

When you buy almost anything from a shop these days the cashier will swipe the product's bar code through the till's scanner. Although this shows the price to be paid, it also records that item of stock as being sold.

In other words, using the scanner to read the bar code is part of the computerised stock control system. It will automatically record that item as being sold and when the stock level reaches the re-order point, new stock will be ordered automatically. What you don't see is that when the stock arrives in the shop it is scanned to automatically update the stock records for the shop. It also shows which items are selling well and which are not. This is helpful in deciding how much of each item of stock to order in future.

ISBN 0-340-90561-1

9 780340 905616

Figure 2.3

Of course, you could use a spreadsheet or database system to record stock movements but the information would have to be entered into the system or spreadsheet manually.

Economies of scale

Economies of scale means the advantages of being big.

This has always been a difficult area for pupils. However, it is in the course and quite often appears in the exam. The best way to tackle this topic is to attempt past paper questions and try to memorise the lists shown below.

Internal economies

Technical economies	Bigger firms can afford to buy more modern and more efficient machinery, and they can afford to carry out research and development to produce new products.
Management economies	The bigger a firm is the more specialised staff it can afford to employ.
	It can appoint its own Accountants and can appoint specialist managers to take charge of departments such as Sales or Human Resources.
Financial economies	Bigger firms find it easier to borrow money from the bank because banks think the risk of non-payment is lower, and they may be able to sell shares on the stock market.
	They can also borrow money at a lower interest rate, which means they have less to pay back.
Marketing economies	The bigger a firm is the more advertising it can afford. Rather than just advertising in local newspapers it can now afford to advertise on television.
Buying economies	They can also buy in bulk, which means they can get discounts for buying more.

Internal economies continued

Risk economies	Big firms can sell to a bigger market and can expand to make different products.
	If sales fall in one area of the market or for one product, the firm can try to increase sales in another area or for their other products.

External economies

In Aberdeen, for example, there are a large number of firms operating in the oil industry. Because there are so many all working in the same sector of industry they can benefit from what we call external economies of scale. External economies are available because of the size of an industry in a local area. External economies come from outside the firm.

External economies available to the oil industry in Aberdeen include:

Figure 2.4 The oil industry in Aberdeen benefits from external economies of scale

◆ There are good local transport facilities (infrastructure) such as road, rail and air links.

◆ Local universities offer a wide range of oil-related qualifications, which makes it easier and cheaper to recruit skilled workers.

◆ There are a lot of workers in the local area who are experienced in the oil industry.

◆ There are lots of specialist suppliers to the oil industry who have located locally.

◆ The area will become well known for its expertise in the oil industry, meaning local oil firms will be able to get contracts world-wide.

All of these will save the firms money by reducing the cost of each product made, and so they may make more profit.

Diseconomies of scale

These push up the costs of each product made and reduce profit levels.

Internal diseconomies of scale

Big firms are harder to manage than small firms. They can easily become inefficient with costs rising and profits falling. The reasons for this are:

◆ Communication between management and workers becomes more difficult which can lead to:

  • delays in production

  • misunderstandings of what is to be done

  • workers becoming unhappy, leading to poor employee relations.

◆ There is a loss of efficiency as managers find it more difficult to keep control of the quality of work done by employees.

◆ Customers get fed up and go elsewhere as they are frustrated with delays in delivery and poor communication.

External diseconomies of scale

If there are too many firms in the same area it may lead to social and economic costs being felt in the local community.

All firms, large and small, can experience problems when too many firms in an industry are crowded into the same area.

◆ Congestion: roads become overcrowded, leading to delays. The same can happen with rail, air and sea travel. All of this can add costs to the business ranging from additional fuel costs as delivery lorries wait in traffic, to lost customers who don't get their order in time.

Figure 2.5 Congestion can add costs to the business

◆ Pollution: heavy, slow traffic creates air pollution, waste from factories increases and the demand for houses leads to overcrowding and destruction of the green belt.

◆ Environmental damage: more green areas disappear to make way for factories, industrial estates, roads etc. This disrupts the local wildlife.

◆ Over-competition: too many businesses chasing the same customers will eventually lead to firms closing down with a loss of jobs and wealth from the local area.

Decision-making Model

This is a topic that pupils either do very well (because they have memorised the steps) or do very badly. Again, there is no easy way to answer questions on this topic – you simply have to memorise the steps. Some pupils find it easier to remember using the mnemonic – POGADSCIE.

I've listed the steps below, so read them a few times and then see how many you can remember!

Key Points

Step 1: IDENTIFY THE PROBLEM
Set the aims.

Step 2: IDENTIFY THE OBJECTIVES
Managers have to decide exactly what it is they want to achieve.

Step 3: GATHER INFORMATION
Good information leads to good decision making. Extensive use of internal and external information is required.

Step 4: ANALYSE INFORMATION
Study the information that has been collected.

Step 5: DEVISE ALTERNATIVE SOLUTIONS
Using the information collected, decide on a number of different courses of action that can be taken to meet the aims.

Step 6: SELECT FROM ALTERNATIVE SOLUTIONS
From the alternative courses of action that have been devised, select the one most likely to meet the aims of the organisation.

Key Points continued ➢

Key Points continued

Step 7: COMMUNICATE THE DECISION
All those involved must know exactly what is going to happen, what effects these changes will have, and why it has been decided to follow this course of action.

Step 8: IMPLEMENT THE DECISION
Arrange for the resources to be put into place.

Step 9: EVALUATE
Take information on how the process is going and compare it to what was expected to happen.

The benefits of using a decision-making model

Time: the process of going through each of the steps means that decisions will not be rushed. Managers will have had enough time to put a great deal of thought into the process. They will have had time to see what needs done and how best to do it, and to evaluate all possible outcomes from the various alternatives.

Quality and quantity of information used: care is taken in gathering, checking and analysing information. Using the best information available gives the best chance of the decision being successful.

Alternative solutions: generating alternatives will allow for some creativity to be included in the decision. It also allows for 'fall back' plans should the original preferred solution turn out to be wrong. Time will be available to assess the consequences of each possible alternative.

Factors of Production

Can you remember what they are? A lot of pupils can't for some reason. You probably covered this at the very start of the course. Even though that will be a long time ago when come to sit your exam, you still need to remember them.

◆ Land: natural resources

◆ Labour: human resources (workers)

◆ Capital: man-made resources

◆ Enterprise: the risk taker who brings the other factors together to produce a good or service.

Internal and External Information

You should remember that:

Internal information comes from within the business (for example, memos, staff newsletters, production reports, budgets, etc.).

External information comes from outside the business (for example, market research, suppliers' catalogues, letters, etc.).

Phone calls and emails can be either internal or external – it depends where they come from.

Influence of Stakeholders

Some pupils find difficulty in understanding the difference between the interest and the influence of stakeholders.

The interest is what they want from the business and the influence is how they can affect the success of the business.

Try to memorise the information in the following table.

Stakeholder	Interest in business	Influence on business
Customers	Want good service and quality goods at reasonable prices	Can buy or not buy the product and can complain
Directors	Make sure that the business continues with success Make sure healthy profits are made and that shareholders (owners) are happy with performance	Make the strategic decisions
Employees	Want job security, good pay and conditions	Can work harder or not, go on strike or take other industrial action, or can leave
Inland Revenue	Makes sure tax rules are followed and all taxes are paid	Can change the amount of tax due to be paid in any year
Managers	Want job security, good salary and benefits, and promotion prospects	Make the decisions that will affect how well the business does

Stakeholder	Interest in business	Influence on business
Shareholders	Want to receive good dividends each year	Can vote at the AGM and can buy or sell their shares
	Want to see the value of their shares rise	
Suppliers	Want repeat orders	Can decide not to supply, change the credit terms, vary the quality of supply
	Want to be paid on time	
Banks	Want to be repaid loans on time	Can alter the interest rates charged
	Want the business to keep within agreed credit limits	Can give or withhold loans

Conflict of stakeholders' interests

It is fair to say that what each of the individual stakeholders wants from the business will have to cause some conflict at some time.

For example, if the directors decide to cut costs by making some staff redundant then this will conflict with the employees' interest in job security.

Or, if the suppliers want to be paid on time this might conflict with the bank wanting the business to keep within its current overdraft limit.

These are both examples of conflict between the interests of the stakeholders.

Sectors of Industry and Sectors of Activity

Here we have a problem. When we talk about sectors of industry, do we mean Private, Public and Voluntary; or do we mean Primary, Secondary and Tertiary?

This question becomes slightly easier at Higher level, where Primary, Secondary and Tertiary are described more fully as the Sectors of Activity, as opposed to the types of business organisation. However, in the 2006 General paper candidates were asked:

'What sector of industry is manufacturing?'

On one hand this question is easy to answer – manufacturing is in the secondary sector. On the other hand some candidates could be confused and say the private sector, as nearly all the manufacturing businesses are privately owned.

Confused?

The problem seems to be that the examiners sometimes use the same term to describe the different descriptions. In the above question it was reasonably obvious what the examiner was looking for, so it will be down to you to read the question carefully and make sure you know exactly what is being asked of you.

Just-in-Time

In the 2006 Credit paper candidates were asked:

'Describe the **advantages** and **disadvantages** of using a just-in-time approach.'

(4 KU)

This question was not done well by many pupils. There could be a number of reasons for this, but probably the main reason was that candidates did not understand what just-in-time (JIT) is about.

This is a popular method of operations for mass manufacturers as it limits the amount of stock held by the organisation to near zero. It works best where there is a very close relationship between the manufacturer and their suppliers.

In practice it is very simple: the stock is held by the supplier and is only brought to the factory as and when it is needed. The whole production process has to be geared to working with the JIT system. The cost savings can be very high as there are none of the following stock holding costs:

◆ Capital tied up in stock: instead money can be used for other purposes or removed entirely from the manufacturer's expenditure.

◆ Storage costs: space, equipment, warehouse and stores staff, services, etc.

◆ Stock losses/wastage: theft, accidental damage, stock exceeding its shelf-life, stock obsolescence.

In a JIT system these costs are paid by the suppliers.

The whole production operation works on the JIT system in that nothing is produced unless there are customers to buy the products. The marketing department will give figures on expected demand or actual orders and only then will production take place.

Supplies are ordered 'just-in-time' to become parts for the final product; these component parts are assembled 'just-in-time' to become finished products; 'just-in-time' to be sold to the customers.

A suitable answer to this question would have been:

The advantages would be:

◆ *up-to-date raw materials*

◆ *less money tied up in stock, which helps with the business's cashflow*

◆ *don't need to pay for storage costs such as warehouse, staff, security, etc.*

◆ *won't be left with worthless stock when it is past its sell-by date, or goes out of fashion.*

The disadvantages would be:

◆ *need very close links with suppliers to ensure they deliver the right materials at the right time*

◆ *production may be held up if deliveries are late*

◆ *can be difficult for a company to meet sudden increases in demand when they don't have stock available.*

The Business Cycle

The business cycle is something that affects the whole of the economy of Scotland.

Sometimes the economy goes through a period of growth or expansion where consumers are spending more money and businesses are producing more goods and services. If the rate of growth is very high we would call this a boom period.

Eventually the economy will start to slow down. Consumers will spend less and businesses will reduce their production. If it starts to slow down very quickly we could have a period called a recession or slump in the economy, where instead of the economy growing, it starts to shrink.

Figure 2.6

Eventually the economy will begin to recover and will go through the whole process again. This is why it is called a cycle.

The cycle is very important because it affects things such as the rate of inflation, the level of employment, interest rates and exchange rates.

It is usually caused by an external factor (PESTEC), which we covered at the start of this book. The most recent slow down was caused by the sharp increase in the cost of fuel and food prices and by problems in the banking industry (the 'credit crunch').

The Euro

The Euro is the single European currency that is used by most of the countries in Europe. Many of the member countries of the European Union, as well as some non-member European countries, decided to get rid of their own currencies and use the Euro.

Figure 2.7 The Euro

This made it easier and cheaper for businesses to trade with one another in different countries. It also made it easier and cheaper for tourists who don't have to change currencies when they travel to different countries.

In Conclusion

I know that this appears to be a long list of problem topics, but remember there are more topics in the exams that have been done well by candidates over the years.

Many of these topics can be used by the examiners to help differentiate between Grade 1 and Grade 2 pupils, and between Grade 3 and Grade 4 pupils, so focusing on them here should help you achieve the higher grade when you sit your exam.

BUSINESS IN SOCIETY

In this chapter we will look at the course content that covers business in society, including the role of business in creating wealth, providing goods and services, and the different sizes and types of businesses.

Business in Society (called Business in Contemporary Society in the National Qualifications) is a very important section of the course. You will cover some of the topics a number of times in the two years of study. If your teacher has taught you in the order of the units shown at the end of this book then you will, for example, cover External Factors (Political, Economic, Social, Technological, Environmental and Competitive) at least three times.

In most cases you will have covered quite a bit of this topic at the start of your course (in Area of Study 1) so by the time you come to sit your final exam it will have been a long time since you studied the topic, apart from revising for your prelim/estimate exam. Therefore, it is very important that you remember to revise this section thoroughly before your actual SQA exam.

There are usually quite a lot of marks for this section in the exam.

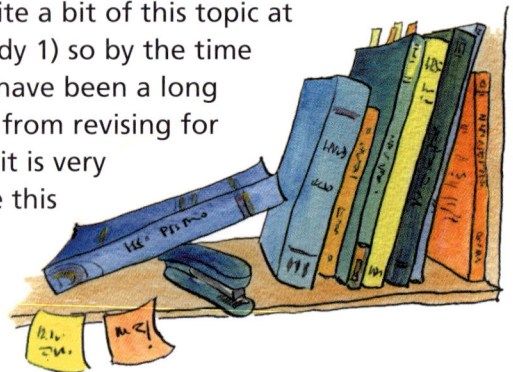

So what is included in the Standard Grade course under Business in Society?

Below is a summary of what is included in this part of the course. This is what you should have covered and have knowledge of by the time of the exam. It is the biggest section of the course and you should expect to see a number of questions on it in the exam paper for each level.

Goods and Services

All businesses are set up to provide either goods or services (and sometimes both) to consumers. The success of the business depends on whether or not the consumer buys or uses these products.

Goods are what we call 'tangible': we can see and feel them. Examples are the book you are reading and the chair you are sitting in.

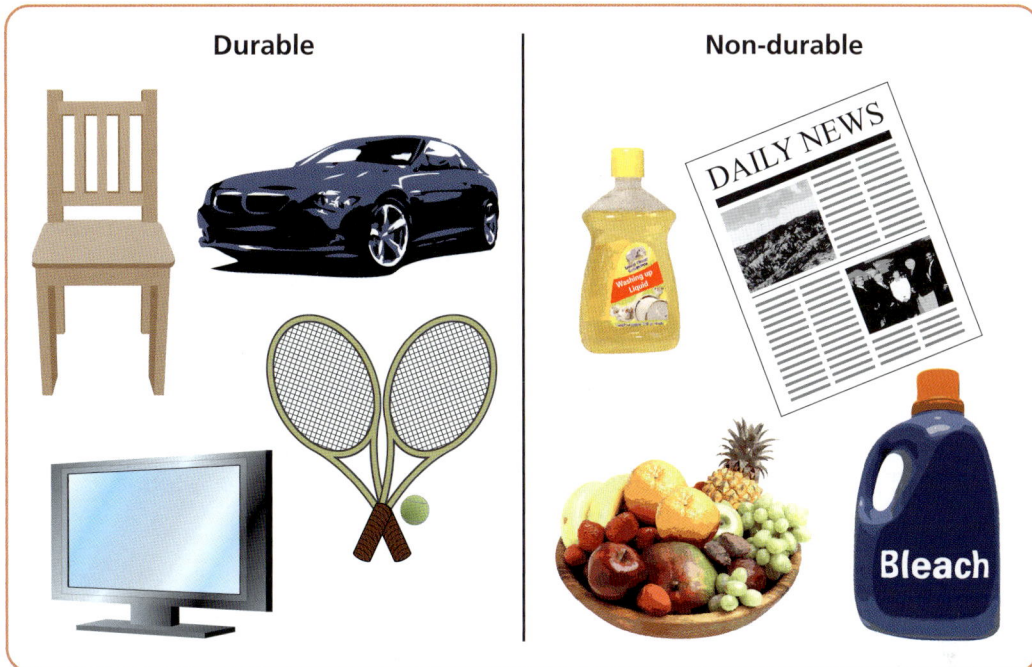

Durable	**Non-durable**

Figure 3.3 Durable and non-durable goods

Durable goods are things that you can use more than once; for example, a television. Non-durable goods are things you would normally only use once; for example, a Mars Bar.

Services are called 'intangible'. These are things that are done for us. Examples are the education that your teachers give you or the NHS (National Health Service). These are both provided by the Government and are in the public sector. Private-sector services include things like retail (shops), tourism, banking, hairdressing, etc.

Sectors of Industry

You should know all about the different types of business that exist. In the private sector you may be asked about sole traders, partnerships and limited companies (both public and private).

You should be able to identify their aims such as survival, profit maximisation, growth, etc., and also how they are managed or controlled and how they can raise finance.

You will have to be able to give the advantages and disadvantages for each type of private business. For example, sole traders make all their own decisions, keep all their own profits and are easy to set up. However, in a partnership you can get extra money into the business, your partner would be able to share the workload, and may have skills that you do not. You would also have someone to cover so you can go on holiday or if you fall sick and are unable to work.

Both sole traders and partnerships have unlimited liability, which means if the business fails they can lose everything, not just what they put into the business. This is why many businesses prefer to become limited companies.

In the public sector you will be expected to know about local government (your council) and central government (Holyrood and Westminster), what sort of services they provide, how they are funded and managed. This would include the NHS, the armed forces, etc. You will also be expected to know about public corporations such as the BBC or the Post Office.

In the voluntary sector you will normally be asked about charities: what their aims are, how they are funded, and how they are owned and controlled.

You may have to give a description and provide examples for each of the business sectors – Primary (the extraction of natural resources, e.g. farming), Secondary (manufacturing, e.g. car producers) and Tertiary (services, e.g. retail).

The Entrepreneur

You must be able to write about what an entrepreneur is and what they do. You should be able to identify the qualities and skills needed to be an entrepreneur. This includes the willingness to take risks, such as the failure of their business and the loss of their investment.

You should also know why they are willing to take risks; for example, to earn more money for themselves, or for the self-satisfaction of being their own boss, or of being successful, and doing something they really enjoy.

You will need to be able to identify sources of finance where the entrepreneur can obtain money to set up their business. These include: their own investment, grants from central and local government, money from friends and family, grants from enterprise bodies, loans from banks and building societies, and overdrafts.

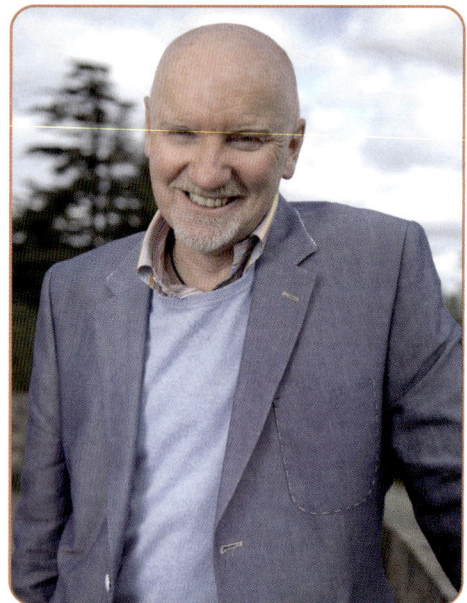

Figure 3.2 Sir Tom Hunter, a successful entrepreneur

The entrepreneur's role includes deciding on a location for a new business; you may be asked about the factors that they will consider when making this decision, including location of raw materials, availability of skilled labour and suitable land, distance to market (bulk reducing, bulk increasing), quality of infrastructure, costs, central and local government assistance, and EU funding.

You may be asked to write about the types of government assistance available for locating in certain areas, including central and local government assistance. You need to know how the government assists businesses to locate and the reasons why they do so; for example, it may be to provide employment and economic growth in a deprived area. You should be able to give an explanation of the types of assistance offered by each of the different organisations.

Creating Wealth

You should know how wealth is created by the production of goods and services, including how businesses add value to their products at each stage of production, and how these goods and services are bought or consumed by consumers in order to satisfy their needs and wants.

Stakeholders

You should be able to identify both the internal and external stakeholders of an organisation, and what their interest and influences are in the organisation.

You should also be able to identify the competing aims of the different stakeholders including: owners, managers, employees, customers, shareholders (existing and potential), providers of finance, suppliers, local community and government (both local and national).

Social and Economic Costs and Benefits

The actions of business will have an effect on the local or national community in which it operates. These effects can be either good (benefits) or bad (costs). You should be able to identify and write about both the social and the economic effects of business on the local community.

Social costs and benefits tend to affect the quality of life within the community; for example, pollution or better roads, etc.

Economic costs and benefits affect the wealth of the community; for example, increased council taxes or greater spending as a result of increased income from jobs, etc.

Factors of production

We have dealt with these earlier in the book, but just to remind you they are: land, labour, capital, enterprise.

Internal and External Pressures (Externalities)

This is a common question in the exam. You should be able to identify both the internal pressures (finance available, resources available, ability of workforce) and the external pressures or influences (political, economic, socio-cultural, technological, environmental and competitive).

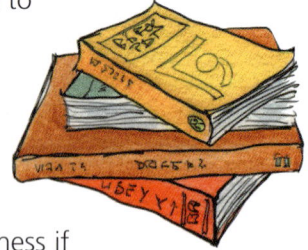

You may well be asked to provide examples of each of the external influences and describe what will happen to a business if they do not respond to these changes. Examples include changes in the business cycle; the effect of economic recession on different types of business; the importance of the European Union, including the single market and the Euro. You must also be able to identify what they should do in each case.

Reasons for Growth and Diversification

Diversification is moving into new markets or new products and you will be expected to identify advantages of diversification such as spreading risk.

You may be asked to write about internal growth, where the business can open new outlets and increase production/sales, and external growth, which can include mergers and takeovers. You will be expected to be able to give examples of both horizontal and vertical integration (forwards and backwards).

Growth of a business will allow it to gain internal economies of scale and you may be asked to identify these and explain why businesses would want to achieve them (lower costs and increased efficiency).

Growth of an industry will allow all businesses in the market to experience external economies of scale; you should know what these are and what effect they can have on the businesses.

Of course, you will also need to know about the diseconomies of scale that can take place when a business or an industry grows too fast, and the inefficiencies that can arise.

Globalisation

Here you should be able to write about the reasons why businesses become global, the problems that arise from operating on a global scale, and why information and communication technology (ICT) is so important to the success of managing a global organisation.

In addition, you may be asked to write about the advantages and disadvantages of multi-national companies, both for the business and for the countries in which it operates.

Revision Questions

Below are some revision questions on the topics covered in Business in Society. To be successful in the exam you should be able to answer most of these. I have also provided answers but please try to answer the questions using your own notes first, and then use the answers to correct them. That way you will have a much better chance of remembering what is in your notes when you are sitting your exam.

Questions

1   Describe two methods of Vertical Integration, giving one advantage for each method.

2   Identify and describe two of the stages in the Business Cycle.

3   Identify three possible aims of a Public Limited Company (plc).

4   What are the external factors that could affect a decision made by a private business?

5   Give two advantages and two disadvantages of a business being a Private Limited Company.

6   Suggest a reason for the conflict of employees and owners as stakeholders in a business.

7   Identify the factors of production that would be needed to set up a new restaurant. Give an example of each.

8   Identify two factors that should be considered when deciding on a location for a restaurant.

9   The restaurant decides to merge with another restaurant. Describe two economies of scale this might bring to the business.

Questions continued ➢

Questions continued

10 Describe the possible effect of the restaurant opening for the local economy.

11 Explain the term entrepreneur.

12 What skills/qualities should an entrepreneur have?

13 Identify the advantages of diversification for a business.

14 Suggest sources of finance for a business.

15 What are the advantages of a partnership?

16 What are the main features of a plc?

17 Identify the benefits and drawbacks of trading with the European Union.

18 Describe the external factors that could affect a business.

19 Explain why a business would want to grow in size.

20 Identify sources of assistance that are available to businesses.

Answers

1 A business can take over another business at an earlier stage in the chain of production – e.g. retailer takes over manufacturer.

The advantages of this are:

It guarantees the supply and quality of raw materials.

The business gets the profits of the supplier.

Economies of scale can be gained.

A business can take over another business at a later stage in the chain of production – e.g. manufacturer takes over retailer.

The advantages of this are:

It guarantees a retail outlet for manufactured goods.

It allows the company to keep control of the marketing of their product.

They may be able to reduce the price of the goods to consumers as the retailer mark-up can be reduced.

Economies of scale can be gained.

They can spread the risk of failure.

Answers continued ➢

Answers *continued*

2 Growth: the economy is experiencing expansion with consumers buying more products and businesses increasing output.

Boom: when the economy grows fast and problems with inflation might occur.

Slow-down: when consumer spending reduces and firms produce less.

Recession/Slump: when the economy has experienced successive periods of negative economic growth.

3 Aims of a plc:

They may seek to grow or expand.

They may want to diversify into new markets or new products.

They may wish to increase or maximise sales.

They may set an aim to increase the profitability of the business.

They could aim to increase their market share.

They want to gain a better reputation and to become more well-known.

They may seek to increase customer satisfaction levels.

They may just aim to survive.

4 Political factors such as changes in the law, e.g. the minimum wage that must be paid to employees.

Social trends such as changes in tastes and fashions that businesses must keep up to date with to ensure they have the products consumers want.

Technological changes such as the growth of e-commerce to stay competitive.

Awareness of the competition: keeping up to date with competitors' products and promotions is essential.

Environmental influences such as climate change, weather problems, pollution.

Economic factors, e.g. unemployment, inflation, interest rates etc.

5 **Advantages:**

All profits can be kept in the family/by the directors of the business.

You can keep control of the business as you have control over who becomes shareholders.

As a limited company you will have limited liability.

Answers *continued* ➤

Answers *continued*

Disadvantages:

Expansion may be more difficult.

There is a lack of funding as you can't raise money on the stock market.

Disagreements/conflicts of interest between the shareholders may arise.

6   The employees may want a pay rise while the owners may want to take more profit from the business.

The employees may want job security whereas the owners may wish to make some workers redundant.

7   LAND: natural resources from farms for the food, gas for the ovens etc.

LABOUR: human resources such as waiting staff, chefs, manager etc.

CAPITAL: man-made resources such as the kitchen equipment, tables and chairs etc.

ENTERPRISE: the owner of the business who set it up.

8   Close to potential customers.

Good suppliers close at hand.

Good parking facilities for customers.

Availability of trained workers.

9   **Internal economies:** more efficient use of staff; bulk-buying of raw materials; easier to get finance; reduction in advertising costs; risk-bearing, managerial responsibilities and technology are shared.

External economies: improved links with suppliers; better distribution of goods; labour supply extended; infrastructure extended.

10 More employment opportunities for the local population.

More spending in local businesses.

More business for local suppliers.

Increase in tax revenues for local council.

Answers continued ➢

Answers continued

11 An entrepreneur is the person who:

comes up with an idea for a business

takes the risks of the venture being unsuccessful

is prepared to finance the venture

brings together the factors of production to achieve business objectives

starts the business

spots a gap in the market.

12 Enthusiasm, risk-taker, persuasive, determination, problem-solving skills, motivational skills, interpersonal skills, decision-making skills, leadership skills, sales/marketing skills, organisation skills, creative, innovative, enterprising, communication skills.

13 Spread the risks of failure when you concentrate on more than one product/market.

Increased sales through new products/markets.

Increased profit.

Economies of scale may become available as the business expands.

14 Sources of finance available would be:

friends and family

bank loan

owners' capital

becoming a partnership or private limited company

building society

venture capital

retained profits.

15 Share the decision making with other partner(s).

Share the workload – you don't have to do everything yourself.

Easier to take time off/more holidays as someone is available to run the business while you are away.

Specialisation can take place by partners in different areas of the work.

Shared responsibility – if the business fails then the debts are split.

Less stressful as you have someone else to rely on.

Answers continued ➢

Answers continued

16 A Public Limited Company (plc):

Is a private-sector business.

Is owned by shareholders.

Trades shares freely on the stock market.

Is run by a board of directors.

Is financed by selling shares on the stock market.

Has limited liability.

Is a separate legal entity from its owners.

Is usually a very large business.

Has to publish its accounts.

17 Benefits:

wider range of products

supplies could be cheaper

taxes on products *could* be less

increased sales

increased market share

increased profits

increased brand awareness

economies of scale

reduced trade restrictions or notes structure

reduced foreign exchange transaction costs.

Drawbacks:

language barriers

cultural differences

different trading laws

transportation problems

increased competition

products may sell at higher prices.

Answers continued ➢

Answers *continued*

18 **Political:** laws imposed by governments on tax, health and safety, wages etc. These increase costs for the business.

Economic: recession and reduced disposable incomes will reduce sales.

Socio-cultural: changing tastes/fashions of consumer.

Technological: changes in technology can lead to increase in production.

Environmental: bad weather affecting delivery/demand for products.

Competitive: competitors bringing out better/cheaper products.

19 To:

increase market share

control market/be market leader

increase sales

improve reputation/become better known

increase profit/profit maximisation

gain economies of scale

control supplies

secure outlets for sales

destroy competition

achieve aims

spread risks.

20 Scottish Enterprise

Locate in Scotland

Local Councils

The Prince's Trust

MANAGEMENT

In this chapter we will look at the content that covers management, including the role of managers, how businesses are organised and controlled, and types of management style.

Although you will learn all about businesses in this course you should remember that the focus is on the management aspect of businesses. One day you may be a manager of some type, in charge of other people, or have responsibility for the success of a business.

The Standard Grade Business Management course teaches you the same sort of things that trainee managers have to learn in order to be successful in industry. You will be asked to make decisions based on what you have been taught or learned, just as managers do in real life.

So what is included in the Standard Grade course under Management?

Below is a summary of what is included in this part of the course. This is what you should have covered and have knowledge of by the time of the exam.

Organisation Structures

How a business is set up and organised will affect how successful it is. There is no single structure that is good for all businesses and you should be aware of the advantages and disadvantages of each type.

You may be asked about tall structures (many layers of management) and flat structures (few layers of management). You should be able to give advantages of each; for example, a tall structure has a high degree of supervision, authority and control, which would be good for an organisation like the army; whereas with a flat structure there is quicker communication and decision-making.

Figure 4.1a Tall organisation structure

Figure 4.1b Flat organisation structure

In a tall structure you tend to find one manager in charge of a few employees (the span of control).

These employees will be supervised closely. In a flat structure there would be a much wider span of control. This gives the workers more responsibility and some decision-making power, which can make their job more enjoyable. Of course, a wide span of control makes the manager's job harder because they have more people to look after.

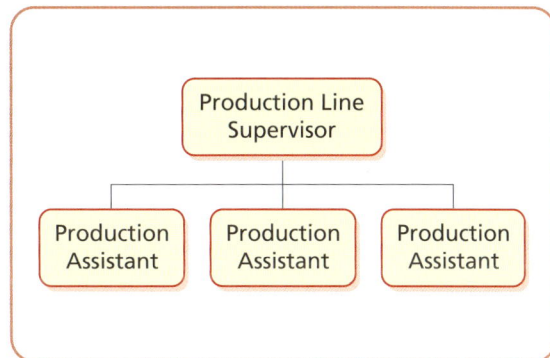

Figure 4.2 Span of control

Small businesses tend to have flat structures because they would not employ many managers or supervisors, whereas large ones would need a lot of people in these positions. You could be asked why a business might choose to restructure; the main reason would be that the business wants to be more efficient and successful, perhaps if they have found that their profits are falling.

Within the structure you should be able to identify both line relationships and functional relationships. Line relationships (who is in charge of who) are about the chain of command and authority and responsibility. Functional relationships (between departments) are about how functional departments work together and how they support the work of the organisation.

Planning and Controlling

In this topic you should know about the importance of planning and control in order to reduce risk. There are a number of ways that a manager can identify and reduce the risks for the business. These will include good financial management, including budgeting and break-even analysis, and where to go to get help and advice outside the business. Preparing a business plan will give the business focus and is very useful when the business needs to obtain additional investment. You should be able to identify what a business plan should include.

You should also be able to identify the benefits of carrying out market research to ensure you are meeting the needs of consumers, including producing a prototype when developing new products.

You may be asked to explain the consequences of poor resource management, which is caused by a lack of management control over the business.

Another common question in this area is about the importance of making good decisions. You may be asked to identify and describe the stages involved in a complex decision-making model, and also the qualities of good information required to make good decisions.

Effective Management

You should be able to identify and describe the main roles of a manager in an organisation, including planning, controlling, leading, monitoring and evaluating. In addition, you need to be able to describe the skills and qualities needed to be a good or effective manager; for example, good leadership skills, good interpersonal skills and good decision-making skills.

Of course, not all managers are the same and you should be able to identify the three main leadership styles: autocratic, democratic and laissez-faire. You may be asked to give the advantages and disadvantages of each style of leadership and how they can affect employee motivation and morale.

Lastly, you should know how working in teams can increase employee motivation and morale.

⇨ **Revision Questions**

Try the revision questions below to see how much you know about the Management topic. Remember: only look at the solutions after you have written your answer.

Questions ?

1 Identify and describe two styles of management.
2 Explain the difference between line and functional relationships.
3 Suggest two ways that a manager can avoid the risk of failure.
4 Identify and describe four steps in a complex decision-making model.
5 Suggest two advantages and two disadvantages of a flat structure for management.
6 Explain how the actions of an autocratic style of manager will affect staff morale and motivation.
7 Identify the qualities of a good manager.
8 Describe the purpose of a business plan.
9 Identify the main titles in a business plan.
10 Explain the term restructuring and give an example.

Answers

1 **Autocratic:** Management make decisions without consulting staff.
   Democratic: Management consult with others before making a decision.
   Laissez-faire: Staff are allowed to make their own decisions.

2 Line relationships refer to the chain of command – who is in charge of who.
   Functional relationships refer to the relationships between departments in the business.

3 Carry out market research.
   Carry out a break-even analysis.
   Prepare a budget.
   Prepare a business plan.

Answers continued ➤

Answers *continued*

4   Identify the problem – set the aims.

Identify the objectives – decide on exactly what it is they want to achieve.

Gather information – collect internal and external information.

Analyse information – study the information they have collected.

Devise alternative solutions – decide on a number of different courses of action that can be taken that will meet the aims.

Select from alternative solutions – select the one that will mostly likely meet the aims of the organisation.

Communicate the decision – inform all staff of the decision.

Implement the decision – arrange for the resources to be put into place.

Evaluate – compare what is happening to what was expected to happen.

5   **Advantages:**

Quicker communication.

Faster decision making.

Disadvantages:

Less supervision.

Greater workload for managers.

6   Workers won't be involved in decision making so will lack motivation.

Their ideas will not be asked for or listened to so morale will be low.

They will not feel involved with or be part of the organisation.

7   **A manager should have:**

good leadership skills

good decision-making skills

interpersonal skills

motivational skills.

Answers *continued* ➤

Answers *continued*

8 A business plan will be drawn up so that the objectives and what will happen in the business are clearly defined. It may also be submitted to potential investors or the bank manager in order to raise finance.

9 Name/address – objectives – location

Type of ownership – number of workers

Key people in the business/job titles – wages and salaries

What will be produced/provided – price

The market

Premises and equipment

Profit estimates – cash flow – capital

10 Restructuring is when the business changes its structure in order to become more efficient.

It could change from a tall structure with many levels of management to a flat structure with fewer levels of management.

MARKETING

Marketing is how the organisation communicates with the consumer. Individual organisations will have different marketing needs. All organisations in the private, public or voluntary sector need to carry out marketing activites to meet their objectives.

Strategic decisions usually involve marketing. For example, to increase market share you have to get customers to buy more of your product and less of your competitors' product. Marketing is the tool that will be used to achieve this.

Using marketing, organisations hope to achieve a number of objectives that are essential for success.

So what is included in the Standard Grade course under Marketing?

Below is a summary of what is included in this part of the course. This is what you should have covered and have knowledge of by the time of the exam.

Markets

You will need to be able to identify and describe market places; for example, outdoor markets, high streets, shopping centres, mail order, Internet websites (e-commerce), etc., and different business markets, whether they are local, national or multinational/global.

Figure 5.1 You must be able to identify different market places

Within each market there will be different market segments and you will be expected to know how these groups are differentiated; for example, by age, gender, income, location, etc. You should also be able to identify why these different segments will want different products and services and how they can be targeted.

The benefits of using market segmentation as part of a business's marketing strategy are that it will allow them to be much more effective and efficient in reaching the consumers at whom their product is aimed.

Market Research

You should be able to identify the purpose of market research and explain the benefits to a business of carrying out market research and the dangers of not doing so. It is an essential part of the planning role of managers.

You should be able to give explanations and examples of both desk research (using existing information: Internet websites, government statistics, newspapers, etc.) and field research (collecting new information: surveys, hall tests, etc.).

You may also be asked to describe the effectiveness of the types of market research within different market segments, and the advantages and disadvantages of different methods of market research.

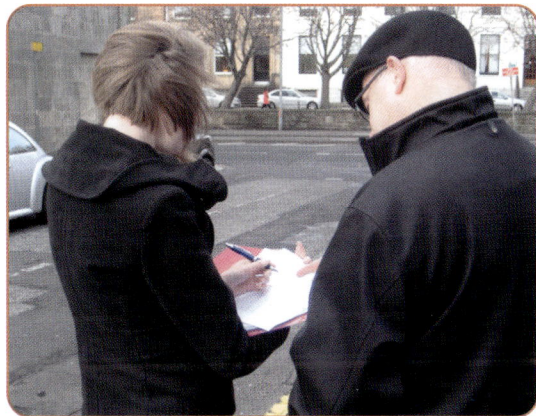

Figure 5.2 Market research questionnaires can be a valuable source of information

Product

You may be asked to explain why innovation (developing new products or new production techniques) is so important to many businesses. Keeping up with, or staying ahead of, the competition is vital to the success of the business.

You should be able to identify and describe the stages involved in product development from generating the new idea to launching it on to the market.

Also, you should be able to explain why some businesses develop new products without carrying out much market research (product led) whilst others spend a lot of time finding out what consumers want before they decide on a new product (market led), giving examples for each approach.

You will be expected to identify and describe the stages in the product life cycle (introduction/launch, growth, maturity and decline), and be able to draw a diagram of the cycle. Particularly important here is your description of what happens to sales and profits at each stage.

You may also be asked to identify the various extension strategies that are available to a business to prevent their product going into the decline stage of the product life cycle. This could include new features/flavours for the product, new packaging, changing price, place or promotion.

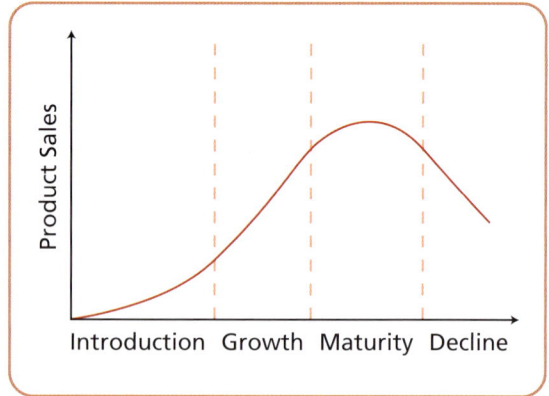

Figure 5.3 The product life cycle

Price

You should be able to explain how businesses can use price as part of their marketing strategy; for example, reducing price in order to increase sales. You may also be asked about the various pricing strategies that can be used and when it would be most appropriate to use them; for example, using penetration pricing to break into new markets, or destroyer pricing to reduce competition.

Promotion

You may be asked to identify various promotional techniques and explain how they would help the business. This could include sales promotions (for example, buy one get one free), advertising campaigns, etc.

In the exam you may be asked about the various types of advertising such as television, national press, local press, radio, leaflets and, of course, the one where more advertising money is now spent – Internet websites.

A business may develop a brand name and you would be expected to identify the advantages to the business of holding a brand name, including customer loyalty and repeat purchases.

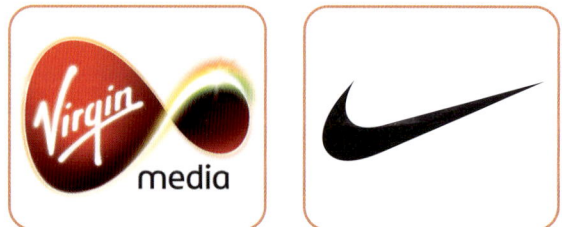

Figure 5.4 Developing a strong brand identity can be the key to business success

Place

Place is about how the product gets from the manufacturer to the consumer. You would be expected to know the different channels and explain when it would be most appropriate to use each one. For example, a small baker may use a direct channel to sell to their customers directly through their shop, whereas Cadbury's would use wholesalers and retailers to make sure that their products get to as many people as possible.

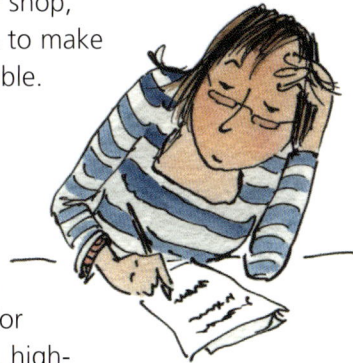

The Marketing Mix

You should understand why it is important to the success of a business that their marketing strategy has the right mix of price, product, place and promotion. For example, it would not be sensible to sell a high-quality, high-price good in Poundstretcher, or for the local baker to advertise on national television. Each of the elements has to be correct for the business to be successful.

Of course, from time to time a business may have to vary one of the elements in the marketing mix that will have an effect on the rest. For example, if their competitors reduce their prices they will have to respond, or, if they decide to produce more of the product, they may have to reduce price, increase production and advertising.

Revision Questions

Attempt the revision questions below and then check your answers against the solutions provided.

Questions

1 Explain the advantages to a business of having a strong brand name.
2 Describe the pricing strategies available to businesses.
3 Give three other marketing strategies that a business could use to increase sales.
4 Explain why a business would sell its products using e-commerce.
5 Describe actions that a business could take to compete effectively in their market.
6 Give reasons why a business would carry out market research.
7 Identify methods of market research.
8 What are the steps that a business should take before launching a new product?
9 Name and describe the stages in a product life cycle.

Questions continued ➤

Questions *continued*

10 Draw a product life cycle diagram.

11 Explain the meaning of product- and market-led approaches.

12 What factors should a business take into account when deciding on a price for their product?

Answers

1 Brand loyalty.

Less need for advertising.

Association with quality.

Ability to charge higher prices.

Enables new products to be introduced easily.

Increases sales/profits.

2 **Penetration Pricing (Introductory Pricing):** Lower price charged at launch of product; price will be increased as sales increase.

Lower price should enable competition to be undercut and persuade customers to try the new product.

Cost-plus Pricing: Price is calculated to be slightly above the cost of production.

Allows the firm to cover its costs and still make a profit until the product becomes more successful.

Competition-based Pricing: Price is linked to be very similar/slightly below that of the main competition.

Allows the business to compete with brand leaders in the market and have the same image of quality etc.

Premium Pricing: Products have a high price.

The product is viewed as an exclusive product so a higher price would be justified to support its brand image.

Destroyer Pricing: Reducing the price so low that competitors are forced out of the market.

Will reduce competition.

Low Price: Business aims to keep the price of the product low to target the low-income market segments.

Customers feel they are getting value for money.

Answers *continued* ➤

Answers *continued*

3   **Alter the product:** new variations, new packaging, variety of sizes, change the name of the product etc.

   Alter the promotion: change the way the product is advertised. Can use TV, radio, outdoor media, print media, celebrity endorsement etc. Or have special offers such as BOGOF, free gifts, competitions etc.

   Alter the place: sell in different locations, use wholesalers, new retailers.

4   Able to reach a wide market (worldwide).

   Customer can shop 24/7.

   Able to reach customers who are unable to get to shop.

   Can target promotions to customers using email etc.

   Payment secured before goods are dispatched.

   Can cut out intermediaries.

   Cuts costs of premises, staff etc.

   Can charge for delivery.

5   Develop new products.

   Update existing products.

   Diversify.

   Lower prices.

   Better quality products.

   Special offers.

   Offer a better service.

   More convenient locations/opening hours etc.

   Have better advertising.

   Merge with another business.

6   Find out if there was a market for the product.

   Find out what price customers were prepared to pay.

   Find out where customers normally shopped/shopping habits.

   Can change the product to meet the needs of customers or improve product or get new ideas for product.

   Reduce business risk.

   Find out about the competition.

Answers continued ➢

Answers continued

7 **Desk Research methods:**

Trade press

Magazines/newspapers

Internet websites

Government statistics

Field Research methods:

Market research agencies

Postal surveys

Surveys/interviews

Consumer panels/focus groups

Hall tests

Observation.

8 Market research gathered to determine consumer demand.

Brainstorming by company to come up with ideas.

Prototype created to test ideas.

Product testing carried out to highlight possible problems.

Test marketing to gather consumer opinion.

Modifications made to prototype.

Marketing campaign decided upon – marketing mix.

Spotting a gap in the market.

Obtaining finance.

9 **Introduction/launch:** product is introduced to/launched on the market. Limited consumer awareness means low sales. Heavy advertising costs to increase consumer awareness etc. Losses are likely to be made at this stage.

Growth: sales are increasing, product awareness is growing, high advertising costs still required to boost performance of product, profits or losses may be made at this stage.

Maturity: sales are levelling out, competition has entered the market, strategies are required at this stage to extend the life cycle of the product, high profits, high costs to keep brand loyalty.

Decline: sales are falling, product is no longer popular, extension strategies need to be employed to inject new life into the product.

Answers continued ➢

Answers continued

10

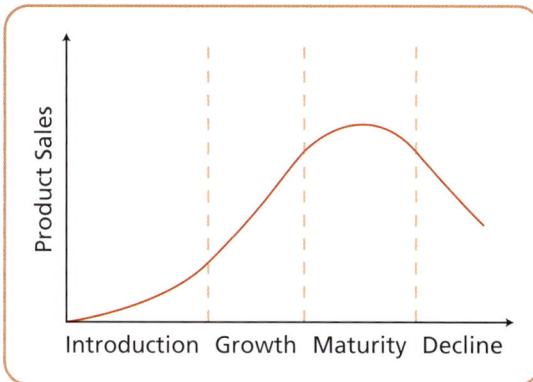

11 A business that is product-orientated is one that designs and makes a product then tries to convince consumers to buy it.

Product-orientated businesses do not look to consumer needs and wants until the final stage – actually selling the product.

A business that is market-orientated tries to find out what consumers need and want before making the product.

These businesses listen to what consumers want in the hope of then developing products that will fully satisfy their needs.

12 Considerations include:

what prices competitors are charging

whether the price charged will cover the costs of production

the quality of the product

the type of market the product is aimed at e.g. designer perfume – the price needs to reflect the 'designer' element and image of the product

how the price charged can be used to increase sales levels

if the price is too high, customers may not buy the product

if the price is too low, customers may get the wrong idea, i.e. poor quality.

FINANCE

The finance function of any modern business plays a vital role in the overall success or failure of the business. It exists to carry out such functions as the maintenance of financial records, payment of bills and expenses, collection of accounts due, monitoring of business funds, payment of wages and salaries, and reporting to management.

Without the money to operate businesses will fail. So it is vitally important to the survival of the business that someone is keeping an eye on the finances, making sure that the business has enough money to meet its aims and objectives.

One of the main roles of the finance function is to provide information to managers and decision-makers within the business.

You will have noticed that quite a lot of the topics covered in Finance appear in the Problem Questions section in Chapter 2. Please do not ignore this area of the course. It could mean the difference between a grade 1 and a grade 2 or a grade 3 and a grade 4, or even a grade 2 and a grade 4, so do yourself a favour and spend some time revising this section. It is a fairly small section of the course, but there will be finance questions in the paper every year.

So what is included in the Standard Grade course under Finance?

Below is a summary of what is included in this part of the course. This is what you should have covered and have knowledge of by the time of the exam. Much of this topic has been covered earlier in the book so we don't need to go into too much detail here.

Business Plan

You should be able to prepare a detailed business plan but, of course, you will not be asked to do this in the exam because you have to do it as part of your Business@Work project. However, as I mentioned under Management, you should know the main sections of a detailed business plan.

Budgeting and Cash Flow

You may be asked to explain the importance of budgeting and cashflow in reducing risk for a business and complete or interpret a simple cash budget. You should also be able to identify ways of overcoming cashflow problems and say when it would be most appropriate for a business to use them.

Break-even Analysis

Here you are most likely to be asked to interpret a graph, give the formula for break-even, or state why it is important to carry out a break-even analysis as part of the planning and controlling of the business.

Final Accounts and Ratios

You will be expected to be able to identify the factors that affect levels of profit and loss: sales, selling price, purchases and expenses. You should be able to complete simple Trading Profit and Loss Accounts and Balance Sheets.

You should know all the ratios covered earlier in the book (see Chapter 2): Gross Profit, Net Profit, Return on Capital, Rate of Stock Turnover and Working Capital. This includes their formulae, what makes them change, and how to use them to compare one year to the next, or one business to the next.

Revision Questions

Now try the revision questions below. When you have completed them compare your answers with the solutions that follow.

Questions

1 Explain the purpose of budgets.

2 Identify methods of reducing costs in a business.

3 Give examples of fixed and variable costs.

4 Identify profitability ratios that a manager may use to monitor the performance of the business.

Questions continued ➤

Questions continued

5 What are the formulae for the following ratios?

Net Profit

Gross Profit

Return on Capital Employed

Rate of Stock Turnover

Working Capital

6 What information is contained in a Trading Profit and Loss account?

7 Identify the main features of a Balance Sheet.

8 What is the formula for calculating the break-even point?

9 Explain the term contribution.

10 Suggest three ways of overcoming a cashflow problem.

Answers

1 To identify inflows and outflows of money on a monthly basis/monitor cashflow.

To enable owner to identify whether costs can be covered/bills paid etc.

To alert owner to any potential problems in cashflow.

To plan finances in advance.

To show to a Bank Manager if applying for a loan.

To allow managers to set targets/compare performance.

2 Find cheaper supplier.

Reduce number of employees/hours worked by employees/make employees redundant.

Prepare a cash budget.

Reduce money spent on expenses such as advertising/promotions, electricity, telephone bills etc.

Just-in-time stock control.

Bulk buying.

Answers continued ➤

Answers continued

3   Examples of fixed costs – rent, insurance, council taxes/rates, loans, advertising, wages, salaries.

    Examples of variable costs – advertising, raw materials, stationery, utilities, telephone, salaries, wages.

4   Gross Profit Ratio.

    Net Profit Ratio.

5   **Net Profit** = (Net Profit ÷ Net Sales) × 100

    Gross Profit = (Gross Profit ÷ Net Sales) × 100

    Return on Capital Employed = (Net Profit ÷ Capital at start) × 100

    Rate of Stock Turnover = Cost of goods sold ÷ Average stock

    Working Capital = Current assets ÷ Current liabilities

6   **Trading account**:

    first part of the final accounts prepared by a business

    shows profit made on buying and selling goods/services

    Sales *minus* Cost of Sales

    calculates **Gross Profit.**

    Profit and Loss account:

    shows the *overall* profit by the business

    Gross Profit – expenses

    calculates **Net Profit.**

7   **Balance Sheet:**

    Fixed assets: Items that are *owned* by the business for more than one year.

    Current assets: Items that are *owned* by the business for less than one year – the value will change.

    Long-term liability: Items that are *owed* by the business and will be paid back over a long period of time, i.e. more than one year.

    Current liability: Items that are *owed* by the business for less than one year.

8   Break-even point = Fixed costs ÷ Contribution per unit

Answers continued ➢

Answers continued

9 Contribution is calculated by: Selling price × Variable cost.

It firstly contributes to paying the fixed costs of the business and then contributes towards the profit of the business.

10 Raising more cash:

Go to the bank and ask for an overdraft or loan.

Sell off assets that the business does not need.

Sell parts of the business (e.g. shares).

Sell its invoices to a debt factoring company.

OPERATIONS

Operations management is concerned with the way organisations produce goods and services. It is a transforming process, turning Inputs (resources) into Outputs (goods and services).

It could be described as the core activity of the organisation, as it actually produces the goods or services for sale. However, marketing could also claim to be the core activity as it achieves the sales that create revenue and profits for the organisation.

So what is included in the Standard Grade course under Operations?

Below is a summary of what is included in this part of the course. This is what you should have covered and have knowledge of by the time of the exam.

Input, Process, Output

Here you may be asked about the operations process and how businesses combine the four factors of production (land, labour, capital and enterprise) to produce goods and services.

The exam paper may include a question about the features of good suppliers or what factors you should consider when selecting a supplier such as price, quality of materials, reliability, discounts, delivery times, etc.

Distribution

You should be able to describe the different methods of distribution of products or services to the consumer. You should also be able to identify the most suitable method of transportation for different goods and services; for example, whether they should use road, rail or air transport. This could also cover the channels of distribution that were discussed in the chapter on Marketing (Chapter 5).

```
                        ┌──────────────┐
                        │   Producer   │
                        └──────────────┘
        ┌────────────┬────────────┬────────────┐
┌────────────┐ ┌────────────┐ ┌────────────┐ ┌────────────┐
│  Consumer  │ │  Retailer  │ │ Wholesaler │ │   Agent/   │
└────────────┘ └────────────┘ └────────────┘ │  Importer  │
                    │              │          └────────────┘
              ┌────────────┐ ┌────────────┐ ┌────────────┐
              │  Consumer  │ │  Retailer  │ │ Wholesaler │
              └────────────┘ └────────────┘ └────────────┘
                                  │              │
                            ┌────────────┐ ┌────────────┐
                            │  Consumer  │ │  Retailer  │
                            └────────────┘ └────────────┘
                                                 │
                                           ┌────────────┐
                                           │  Consumer  │
                                           └────────────┘
```

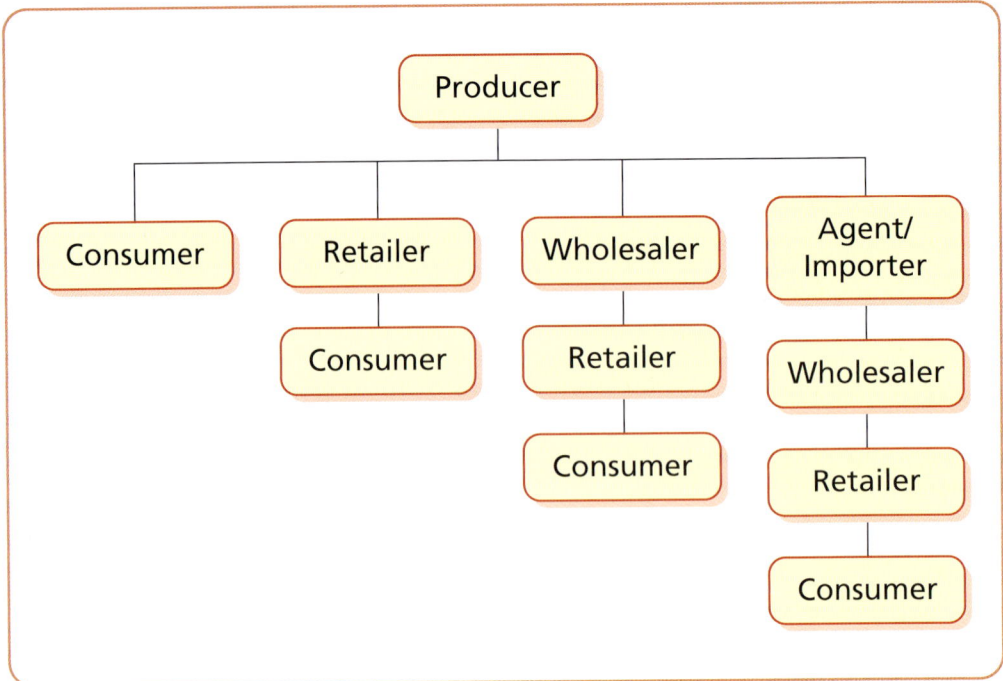

Figure 7.1 Channels of distribution

Types of Production

The three main types of production are covered in the course: job, batch and flow production. You should be able to describe the key features of each. For example, job production is a 'one-off' production that can be tailored to the customer's exact requirements and is usually more expensive. It will normally use skilled labour rather than machines, making it a high-cost method of production.

You should be able to give examples of products manufactured under each process and the advantages and disadvantages of each type of production process. For example, car producers such as Ford would use flow production because they are a mass manufacturer.

The main advantage is lower unit cost of production; the main disadvantages would include the fact that it is very expensive to set up a car manufacturing plant and it is not possible to produce a car to the individual customer's specification.

Figure 7.2 Flow production

People v. Machines

You need to understand the difference between mechanisation (the use of machines in the production process) and automation (replacing workers with robots or computer-controlled machines).

Exam questions are likely to focus on the advantages and disadvantages of both labour- and capital-intensive production and where products and services can be improved through technology.

You may also be asked to identify the advantages and disadvantages of using people and/or machinery in the production process and the effects on the workforce of introducing automation/computerisation to the production processes. These could include loss of jobs, need for additional training or training for new jobs.

Figure 7.3 An automated production line

Figure 7.4 Labour-intensive production

Stock Control

In the exam you could be asked questions about the necessity of good stock control systems to ensure the business's success. The business needs stock in order to provide products for their customers. If their stock control is poor they will lose orders to competitors and consumers will lose confidence in the business due to their failure to deliver.

The main issues you need to be concerned about are the security of stock and security systems; computerised and manual stock control systems for keeping records of stock bought and used; and the storage of stock to ensure it does not deteriorate, go out of fashion, or go past its sell-by date.

You should also be able to identify, describe and explain just-in-time production, including advantages and disadvantages. This was covered earlier in the book (see Chapter 2) .

Quality Measures

You may be asked to explain the reasons why producing a quality product/service is an important aim for many businesses and also the factors that should be considered, including the quality of raw materials, the quality procedures used in production and the quality of the after-sales service.

You should also be able to describe the main measures of quality used in business such as Quality Circles, Total Quality Management, Quality Control and Quality Assurance. You will probably be asked about their main features and the advantages and problems that can arise when a business introduces a system of quality.

Customer Service

Here you should know the various methods of monitoring customer satisfaction with the service provided and how customer service can be improved. Remember, good customer service will increase reputation and reduce customer complaints and returns.

Revision Questions

Try to answer the following questions using your own notes and then check your answers against the solutions that follow.

Questions

1. Name and describe a method of production for a food manufacturer. Identify two problems of using this method.
2. Describe why a business would invest in robotics for production.
3. Identify when a business would use labour-intensive production.
4. Explain how a business can ensure a quality service for its customers.
5. Describe the advantages and disadvantages of using skilled workers.
6. Identify ways in which a business can ensure quality in its production process.
7. What does the term mechanisation mean?
8. What factors should a business consider when selecting a supplier?
9. Explain the benefits of a system of computerised stock control.
10. Explain the term 'Quality Circle'.

Answers

1 **Flow/Mass/Line Production**

Products made in continuous flow on production line/in stages.

All products same/standardisation.

Capital-intensive production/automation methods used.

OR

Batch Production

Products made in batch *at same time* before another batch started.

Variety of flavours produced in batches.

Problems:

Flow Production

Expensive outlay for equipment.

Constant maintenance required.

De-skilling of staff.

Possible redundancies.

Low staff morale.

Whole line must be stopped when problems are found.

Mistakes can go un-noticed causing wasted products.

Batch Production

Adaptable equipment required.

Careful planning of ingredients needed.

Mistakes can ruin a whole batch of goods.

Equipment needs to be cleaned between batches.

2 Faster production.

Higher quality output.

24/7 working.

Can do boring and repetitive tasks.

Less expensive than employees.

Can be more reliable than employees.

Answers continued ➢

Answers continued

3 When the type of technology required is not yet available.

  When the cost of using machinery would be more expensive than using employees.

  When they want to provide jobs (have been given incentives by government for job creation).

  When they want employees to do quality checks before despatching goods (which machines cannot do).

4 Polite and friendly attitude of staff.

  Good returns policy.

  Trained employees.

  Applying for Quality Standards (e.g. IIP, BSI, ISO).

  Using quality assurance or quality control.

  Quality Circles.

  Provide a customer helpline/good after-sales service.

5 **Advantages:**

  Can adapt the product to suit customer requirements.

  Ability to do detailed work that a machine cannot do.

  Increase in the quality of the product because it is made by skilled craftsmen.

  Can demand a higher price because it is made by skilled craftsmen.

  Gives company a better image.

  Less wastage.

  Good reputation.

  Don't have to spend money training workers.

  Disadvantages:

  Cost – wages.

  Skills shortages – harder to find skilled workers.

  Re-training may be needed.

  Can be less accurate than machines.

6 Use staff appraisal to motivate workers.

  Buy quality raw materials.

  Train workers.

Answers continued ➤

Answers continued

Implement TQM.

Implement Quality Control/Assurance.

Update machinery/maintenance of machinery.

Use Quality Circles.

Recruitment – good quality employees.

Use Benchmarking.

7   Machinery/equipment or technology being used to make the product.

8   Alternative suppliers – should they use a local or a large national supplier?

Delivery time – how long will it take between ordering and receiving the supplies?

Price – do they offer discounts, free delivery?

Quality – can they offer the consistent quality required?

Quantity – can they offer the amount required?

Storage facilities – how much can the business store if bulk buying?

9   **EPOS system**

Bar coded stock items.

Scanner used to record stock movements.

Automatic updating of stock records.

Can be used to record stock automatically.

OR

Spreadsheet system/Database system (accept names of packages)

Column entries for stock received, stock issued.

Balance column to record stock movements.

Formulas used to carry out calculations.

Graphs can be produced to show stock movements.

10 **Quality Circles:** Quality Circles are groups of people that meet regularly within the organisation to identify, discuss and resolve problems in the production process.

Members of the Quality Circle should include a wide range of people from the workforce from shop-floor workers up to senior management.

HUMAN RESOURCES

The people that work for an organisation represent a big investment for their employers in terms of time and money. Through the jobs that they do, each and every employee makes a contribution towards the organisation achieving its objectives.

Employees are resources of the organisation and Human Resource Management aims to make the most efficient use of these resources, as the better the employees are at their job and the harder they work, the more successful the organisation will be.

So what is included in the Standard Grade course under Human Resources?

Below is a summary of what is included in this part of the course. This is what you should have covered and have knowledge of by the time of the exam.

Why People Work

For this topic you should have a good understanding of what motivates people to work. The obvious reason is to earn money but people gain more than just money from a job and few people will stay in a job they do not like. For example, the job might give them personal satisfaction or it might allow them to be creative and use their skills. They will gain a feeling of security and will have the opportunity to meet more people and make more friends. It is important for managers to understand these other motivations so that they can get the most out of their staff.

Recruiting the Right Person for the Job

You should know all the steps that are taken in the recruitment and selection process. This will include how to identify that a vacancy exists, how to prepare a job description/specification and an advert for a job, and the various ways that the job can be advertised. For example, if you wish to recruit internally you could use the staff newsletter or notice board; if you are recruiting externally you could use an agency to find the right person, or advertise in newspapers, on-line, at Job Centres, etc. You may be asked to give the advantages of both internal and external recruitment.

You should also understand the process of identifying what qualities, skills and qualifications are required for the job using a person specification. These will be used to compare with the application forms when deciding who will be invited to interview.

It is not uncommon to be asked to identify and describe the various working hours and types of employment that can be offered, such as full-time, part-time, permanent, temporary, contract and casual working. You should also be able to answer questions on flexi-time and job sharing. You could be asked about the various types of worker such as skilled/professional, unskilled/manual, semi-skilled, etc.

Figure 8.1 External recruitment

Figure 8.2 External recruitment

Another area that you might be asked to write about is the contracts of employment that will be issued to the new employee. You should be able to identify what the contract will contain, such as place of work, working hours, holiday entitlement, etc.

Training and Appraisal

Questions here could include the identification and description of the different types of training. These include induction training for the new employee, on-the-job training (where the person is trained while actually doing the job), off-the-job training (where they are trained away from their workplace) and apprenticeships.

Again, you will be expected to know the advantages and disadvantages of each, and also the reasons for re-training and upgrading the skills of employees.

You may need to answer questions on the role of appraisal for staff motivation and target setting. You should be able to describe both formal and informal appraisal, and the advantages and possible disadvantages of appraisal.

Inter-relationship Between Employees and Employers

This could include questions on the role and purpose of Trade Unions, as well as methods of Industrial Action that are available to employees and how each of these will affect the employer (lower production/sales, etc.). You should be able to describe the role of ACAS in helping resolve industrial disputes.

You will need to know about the different types of legislation affecting employment including the various forms of discrimination (race, gender, disability, age, etc.) and the employment protection legislation in the various employment acts.

The pieces of legislation most commonly asked about are the Equal Pay Act, Health and Safety at Work Act, Sex Discrimination Act, Race Relations Act, Employment Acts and the Minimum Wage Act.

Figure 8.3 Industrial action

You should also know how things like team working, Quality Circles and works councils can help keep good relations between employees and employers.

Changing Patterns of Employment

Here you will be expected to know the reasons for moves towards new working practices and industries; for example, the decline of manufacturing and the increasing growth of the service sector.

The most common approach for questions about flexible working practices ask for a description of and the advantages and disadvantages of flexi-time, home working, teleworking, core staff, casual staff, job sharing, and how ICT has helped these develop.

Revision Questions

Try the following questions to help you revise this topic and then check your answers against the solutions that follow.

Questions

1   Name and describe two forms of industrial action that employees might take when in dispute with their employers.

2   Name the type of training given to new employees.

3   How can a business motivate employees?

4   Identify reasons why there has been an increase in the number of part-time and temporary workers in recent years.

5   Describe the steps in the recruitment process.

6   Suggest ways in which a business can develop its employees.

7   Identify the main pieces of employment legislation.

8   Explain why some businesses prefer to recruit internally.

9   Identify methods of external recruitment.

10 Identify the advantages and disadvantages of external recruitment.

11 Identify the items that should appear on a contract of employment.

12 Identify the information that should be included in a job description.

Answers

1   Go on strike – employees withdraw their labour and refuse to carry out any work

Work to rule – employees work to the terms of their contract only and do not carry out any additional duties

Overtime ban – employees refuse to undertake any overtime in the company

Sit-in – workers occupy the premises to disrupt work from taking place in the factory

Go slow – employees carry out duties as slowly as possible

Boycott – employees refuse to carry out a particular task

2   Induction training

Answers continued ➤

Answers continued

3 Set targets

Financial – salary/bonus payments/productivity payments/overtime

Praise

Delegated tasks/empowerment

Training

Job enrichment/job enlargement/job rotation/team working

Staff appraisal

Quality Circles

Promotion

Consultation with employees

Good working conditions

4 Businesses do not want to pay out as much in pensions

Changes in demand

Uncertain markets (sales vary)

Firms wanting to cut wage bills

More flexible workforce for firms

Workers prefer flexibility in employment

5 Job analysis

Job description drawn up

Person specification drawn up

Job advert prepared

Job advertised

Applications/CVs received

Short listing carried out

Interview questions prepared

Referees contacted

Candidates invited for interview

Successful candidate informed

Unsuccessful candidates informed

Answers continued ➢

Answers continued

6 Training – gives employees better skills

Appraisals – gives employees chance to give opinions and enables targets to be set

Incentives – e.g. bonuses can encourage staff to work towards aims

Good communication between staff – managers communicating aims with employees effectively should ensure that these are achieved

Internal promotion – giving employees more responsibility to enable them to have more influence on the decisions made in the business

Team building – allows employees to feel valued and motivated

Involvement in decision making

Involvement in TQM

Job rotation

7 Equal Pay Act

Disability Discrimination Act/Disabled Persons Act

Race Relations Act

Employee Protection Act

Sex Discrimination Act

Unfair Dismissal Act

Minimum Wage Act

Maximum Working Hours Directive

Human Rights Act

Health and Safety at Work Act

Data Protection Act

Employment, Equality and Religious Orientation Act

8 Staff already known

Training has been given

Reduce costs

Increase in motivation

Loyalty of staff

Saves time in the recruitment process

Promotion prospects for staff

Answers continued ➢

Answers *continued*

9   Job Centre

Advertise in newspaper

Trade journals

Employment agency

Head hunting

TV/radio

10 **Advantages:**

Larger selection of applicants

New employees bring fresh ideas

External person more suitable for job

Person appointed has a proven record

Disadvantages:

Training will be required

Expensive to advertise

Lowering of staff morale within the organisation

11 Job title

Personal details

Name of business

Contract terms

Duties relating to the job

Hours of work

Holiday entitlement

Sick pay and allowances

Discipline/grievance procedure

Date employment began

Rate of pay/how they will be paid, e.g. weekly/monthly

Pension scheme

Notice required

Answers *continued* ➢

Answers continued

12 Job title

Purpose of the job

Specific duties

Responsibilities

Location of job

Person responsible to/for

Hours of work

INFORMATION AND ICT

The course should provide you with the opportunities to acquire skills and confidence in the use of information technology to handle, present and interpret data in realistic business contexts, and to use business applications to aid decision making in real-life, simulated and computer-based learning situations.

So what is included in the Standard Grade course under Information and ICT?

Below is a summary of what is included in this part of the course. This is what you should have covered and have knowledge of by the time of the exam.

Types of Information

The main types of information are written, numerical, verbal and graphical/pictorial. You should be able to give examples of each and say when it would be most appropriate to use them.

Figure 9.1 You should be aware of the different types of information

Using Computers to Generate Information and Communicate

Here you will be asked about the various types of hardware and software that businesses use. You could be asked to identify them and give the advantages and disadvantages of each, as well as when it would be most appropriate to use them.

The software packages that you will be asked about will be word processing, spreadsheets, databases, desktop publishing, graphics software, Internet websites (including the features of a good website), email and presentation packages such as PowerPoint.

The hardware covered could include fax machines, video conferencing, voice mail, mobile telephones/ text messaging, pagers, telephone and computer networks.

Importance of Good Communications

You should know about the problems that can arise as a result of poor communications, as well as the features of good information such as timeliness, accuracy, relevance, cost effectiveness and completeness of the information.

Questions could include the purpose of communication, the various methods of communication and how a mix of

Figure 9.2 Video conferencing

methods of communication may be used in a given situation. You will also be expected to know the barriers to effective communication.

Internal and External Sources of Information

You may be asked to identify and describe the types of internal (generated within the organisation) and external (generated outside the organisation) information that businesses gather, as well as how they use this information, giving examples of each type.

You will also be expected to describe formal and informal information, their uses and value.

Using Information to Monitor and Control Businesses

Managers need good information in order to make good decisions about how best to achieve the objectives of the business. You may be asked about the ways in which managers use information to aid decision making, planning and controlling.

This could include: using accounting information to compare performance over a period of time; using feedback from customer surveys to improve quality of service/product provided; using sales records to see if targets were met and to decide what action needs to be taken; and using break-even information to decide on selling prices, production levels, etc.

Revision Questions

Below are some revision questions for this chapter. Again, please try to answer them using your notes before you look at the solutions.

Questions

1 Give examples of internal and external information that is used in a business.
2 What features should a business include on its website?
3 Give examples of problems that customers might face when using a website.
4 Identify ways that a business could use ICT to communicate with their customers.
5 What ICT could a Sales Representative use to work away from the office?
6 Explain how ICT has increased the number of homeworkers.
7 Explain how ICT can be used effectively in finance.
8 What are the qualities of good information?
9 Identify the possible drawbacks of using ICT.
10 Identify the main types of information and give an example of each.
11 Explain how ICT can help managers.

Answers

1   Internal Information

Sales records

Financial information

Market research information gathered by the company

Business plan

Internal emails

Minutes from meetings

Company newsletters

External Information

Information about competitors

Information from market research companies

Government statistics

Consumer surveys

Newspaper articles

Information from suppliers

2   It should be easy to navigate and find what you are looking for.

Essential information should be displayed clearly – name, address, telephone and fax numbers, products and prices etc.

Hyperlinks should be available to related websites.

Colour/animation can be used to highlight essential features.

Secure/padlock area for paying for goods.

E-commerce facilities to buy or order on-line.

It should be regularly updated and all information should be up to date.

A search facility should be available.

Feedback forms allow the company to obtain useful information from their customers.

They should have a web address that is easy to remember/spell.

The site should have a FAQs (Frequently Asked Questions) section – to allow customers to ask questions and get feedback.

It should include a product catalogue for customers to view products before ordering.

Answers continued ➤

Answers *continued*

3   Computer crashes

Using incorrect web address

Information has not been updated

Too many pop-ups

Lack of personal contact with business

Viruses

4   Internet website/pop-ups

Email

SMS messaging service/text messages

Plasma screen/computerised billboards/computerised digital displays

Video conferencing

Fax

5   Equipment: laptop/PalmPilot, PDA, mobile telephone, fax, pager etc.

Software: e-diary, word processing, spreadsheet, database, PowerPoint, email, Internet browser

6   Broadband has allowed homeworkers to do work at home that they would previously have had to do in the office.

It is a fast, secure and efficient system.

They can use email and web conferencing to keep in touch with other staff.

Work can be downloaded immediately.

7   Spreadsheets can be used to record all financial transactions.

Calculations can be carried out automatically using formulae.

Different spreadsheets can be linked together to update all financial information simultaneously.

'What-if' analysis can be carried out to help with decision making.

Graphs can be created to make financial information easier to understand.

Answers *continued* ➢

Answers continued

8 Good quality information should be:

Accurate – no errors

Timely – up to date and available when needed

Complete – there should be nothing missing

Relevant – should be about what you need to know

Available – should be readily available when needed

Cost-effective – shouldn't cost too much to obtain

Objective – free from any bias

Concise – has to be understood easily and quickly by the decision-maker

9 Initial training in using ICT is expensive and time consuming.

Can be difficult to keep up to date with ICT as software/hardware is constantly changing.

Individuals may feel they have become isolated from human contact, e.g. automated telephone answering services means receptionists are no longer needed.

Health problems have been linked to using ICT for long periods of time, e.g. eyestrain, RSI (repetitive strain injury), back problems etc.

Dependence on use of ICT means that in the event of breakdown or power cuts problems will arise!

10 Verbal (oral) – e.g. phone call

Paper-based (written) – e.g. letter

ICT-based – e.g. email

Numerical – e.g. financial accounts

Pictorial/graphical – e.g. an organisation chart

11 Generating information quickly

Providing accurate information

Storing large amounts of useful information

Monitoring and controlling

Decision making

Measuring performance

Identifying new business opportunities

PRACTICAL ABILITIES PROJECT

Practical Abilities

The course should develop practical abilities through:

◆ using a range of information and information technology in business contexts

◆ participating in business simulations

◆ applying business techniques in a variety of contexts

◆ accessing real-life business enterprises for information.

The Business@Work simulation may seem a bit dated now but it is still one of the few examples of this type of assessment. And where else would you get the chance to play a game for a grade in your exam?

During your course your teacher will hopefully have given you at least a couple of opportunities to use the software and learn its various functions. This is important because it should be relatively easy for you to get a very good grade in this element if you are willing to make the effort.

The Practical Abilities Project is an 'open book' assessment, which means you can use your course notes and the information contained within the software to answer the questions asked. So in theory you should get full marks.

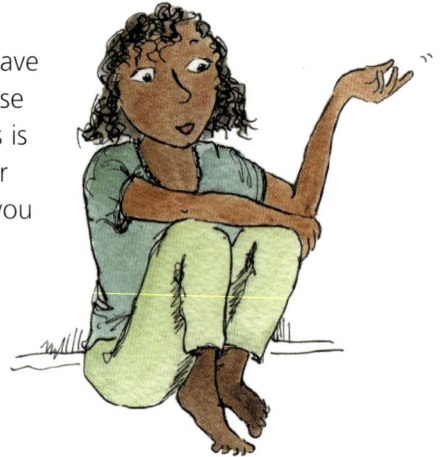

Sometimes a pupil will sit the Practical Abilities Project at Credit Level and the external paper (the exam) at General Level.

The main reason for a low grade in the project is because pupils don't read carefully what they are being asked, nor are they willing to make the effort to get all the marks available. I will try to help you with this in this chapter.

You will complete the project over a number of weeks, so you will have the opportunity to change your answers if you find a better or more detailed answer. Certainly, before you hand it in you should take time to check you have completed every question, have all the correct printouts, and have matched the number of points you have given to the number of marks available.

Your teacher is allowed to give you some guidance but is not allowed to help you answer the questions. Nor are your fellow pupils – it must be all your own work.

Once you have finished, your teacher will mark your script and then submit a grade for you to the SQA. This might not be your final grade because each year some schools are asked to submit a sample of scripts to the SQA for a process called verification. This just means that they are checking that your teacher has marked it correctly. You should not worry about this too much because the vast majority of schools are now very good at marking this paper.

The Practical Abilities Report

The report is split into three sections. The first section is normally about using the Business@Work software and tries to relate in some way to the second section. The other two sections deal with specific areas of the course you have been studying.

For example, Section 1 of the 2008 General Project asked about the tools you would use for selecting the site of the business and Section 2 was about location. Similarly, at Credit Level, Section 1 was about site selection and Section 2 was about Business Decisions, with some of the questions based around the location decision. (For the past three years the second section at Credit Level has covered Business Decisions.) Section 3 of the 2008 General Project covered Growth and at Credit Level covered E-commerce and Globalisation.

At Foundation and General Level you are given a report to complete. At Credit Level it is good practice to word process your report so that you can go back and amend or edit your answers without having to re-write your report every time.

Figure 10.1 The Business@Work office

Section 1: Using Business@Work

This section covers your knowledge and understanding of the software used in the simulation and usually focuses on one of the tools available to you, which are:

◆ The start-up file

◆ Map of Mereside

◆ PC

◆ PDA (Personal Digital Assistant)

◆ Toolbar

◆ To Do List

The start-up file

You are buying the stationery business from Marie and she has provided a lot of useful information that you will need to complete the game and the report.

It is important to read through this file and make a note of all the information it contains before you start running the simulation.

When my own pupils are playing the game and they ask where they get a piece of information from, it can usually be found in the start-up file.

Map of Mereside

The map gives detailed information about each of the areas of Mereside and should be used when deciding where to locate your business. Each of the maps has a number of layers, which you can access by clicking on each in turn. There are also a number of video clips available that give more information on Mereside.

PC

The icons in the PC give information on the following:

Market Research	Here you can see the results of any market research questions you have bought during the simulation.
	Useful for adjusting your prices/marketing during the game.
Site Planner	Gives details of each of the sites you can choose for your business, along with financial information such as rent, alterations and amount of bank loan. Very helpful when deciding on a site and for completing your business plan.
Production Planner	This helps you decide how much to produce, what prices to charge, and also helps avoid paying overtime unnecessarily.
Internet	This gives you access to BusinessWorks.com, a very useful site with a lot of theory and useful information to help you complete your project report.

Email	This lets you know what is happening in the business environment so you can adjust your production or price during the game to make the best profits.
View/Print Reports	You will need to use this for some of the printouts asked for in the project, e.g. To Do List, Profit and Loss Account, Cash Budget, etc.

PDA (Personal Digital Assistant)

This allows you to record notes during the game. It is particularly useful when completing your business plan and running the simulation, as you can have it open when transferring information about your site or production planner to the business plan.

Some of my own pupils like to write this on paper but in 2007 Section 1 was about using the PDA so it makes sense to make as much use of the feature as you can so that you can answer the questions correctly.

The PDA also includes a calculator function to help with your decisions.

Toolbar

This gives you quick access to some of the other tools available to you.

To do list

This is where you access the game. You have to complete each of the steps in the list in turn. Generally speaking you cannot go back once you have completed one of the items on the To Do List, so please make sure you are happy with your decision before you complete the task.

It is very important that you are familiar with the game simulation before you undertake the actual project, otherwise you will have difficulty completing Section 1 and will lose marks unnecessarily.

Section 2: Business decisions

As I have said before, this section usually relates in some way to Section 1.

For example, in the 2008 Credit Paper Question 6 (b), pupils were asked to identify the key stages in the complex decision-making model and to relate them to the location decision for the site.

There were 10 marks available here: 5 for the correctly identified stage in the decision-making model, and 5 for relating them to the location decision. Most of my pupils could identify 5 stages but had difficulty in relating them to the location decision.

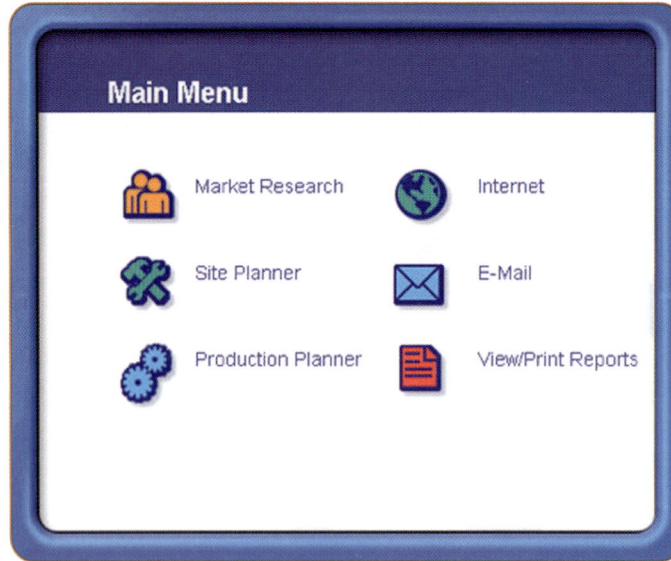

Figure 10.2 Make sure you know how to use all the game tools

What they should have written was:

Stage	Relation to the location decision
Identify the problem	You need to find a site for the business in Mereside
Identify the objectives	Find the most suitable site that will allow you to operate successfully
Gather information	Get the information available from: BusinessWorks.com Map of Mereside Start-up file Site planner Video clips
Analyse	Study the information and decide what is relevant
Devise alternative solutions	Pick the sites that would be suitable
Select from alternatives	Pick the site that suits best

Not all of the questions in Section 2 will relate to Section 1, but they will relate to some of the decisions you have made in the game. For example, in the 2008 Credit paper Question 8, the pupils were asked to explain the term 'capital expenditure'. The question stated that this represented the items that they had bought from Marie for the business, and pupils were asked to give a further example. Many pupils found it hard to find an answer in their course notes and decided to use Google to try to find a suitable answer. Unfortunately they accepted the first answer that was given but it did not relate to the question that was being asked. So if you are looking up information from other sources, please make sure that the source is reliable and the answer you give relates to the question.

Of course, the answer should have been: Capital expenditure is spending on fixed assets. An example would be a delivery van.

Section 3

This also relates to the simulation but in a much more general way. The questions asked here are similar to those asked in the exam, although they relate to both the simulation and a short case study provided in the report.

You should use your course notes and any other resources available to you to help you complete the report and get as many marks as possible. Remember there is only 1 mark between a Grade 1 and a Grade 2, and 1 mark between a Grade 3 and a Grade 4.

The marks you achieve in the project report have no relation to how well you do in the game. It doesn't matter if you made fantastic profits or terrible losses as this will not affect your grade. Of course, being Business Management students you will want to do as well as possible and your business to be a success.

Summary

- Make sure you have practiced the game before you start to complete your project.
- Always read Marie's file carefully before you begin.
- Make sure you know how to use all the game tools properly, and have a note of the information and functions they contain.
- Complete your report as you play the game – don't try to do one and then the other.
- Make sure you hand in correct versions of all of your printouts.

Summary continued ➤

Summary *continued*

◆ Give enough answers to get all the marks available in each question – do a little bit more to be safe.

◆ Make sure you have not missed out any questions.

◆ Use all the notes etc. available to you so that you write the correct answers.

◆ Don't hand in your report until you have checked it through thoroughly.

◆ Remember, you should have plenty of time to complete the report so do as much as you can.

APPENDIX

The following tables show the course content in each of the four areas of study, as specified by the SQA.

Area of Study 1: What is business?

Foundation Level	General Level	Credit Level
1.1 What do businesses do?		
Goods and services	Range of goods and services	Satisfaction of wants
Difference between small and large businesses	Private, public, government, voluntary sectors	Production and consumption
Charities	Primary, secondary, tertiary business sectors	Creating wealth
1.2 Why do businesses exist?		
Enterprise	Concept of entrepreneurship	Risk taking
Profit		Social costs and benefits
Charity	Aims of business (relative to different types of organisation) and stakeholders	Economic costs and benefits
Public service		
1.3 How are businesses organised?		
Simple organisation structures	Different organisation structures	Span of control
Four functional areas	Impact of size on structure	Functional relationships
	Line relationships	Difference between authority and responsibility

Appendix

Area of Study 2: How do businesses develop and perform?

Foundation Level	General Level	Credit Level
2.1 How do businesses start?		
Need for enterprise	The marketplace	Researching the market
Identify needs	External information and advice	Calculating risk
Buyers and sellers	Identifying risk	Detailed business plan
Help – where to get it	Characteristics of factors of production	
Taking risks		
Completing a simple business plan	Preparing a simple business plan	
2.2 How do businesses grow?		
Successful product/service	Diversification	Research and development (product and market)
Expand sales	Innovation	Reasons for growth
Takeovers/mergers	Horizontal and vertical integration	
2.3 How do businesses survive?		
Need to plan	Planning and controlling	Market research
Saleable products/services	Awareness of budgeting and cashflow	Evaluation and comparison
Covering costs	Using final accounts	Using final accounts and ratios
	Calculating and interpreting simple ratios	
2.4 Why do businesses fail?		
Competition too fierce	Not moving with times	Business cycle
Recession	Role of competitors	Response to change
Cashflow problems	Simple analysis of final accounts	Externalities
		Poor resource management
2.5 What is a successful business?		
Achieving objectives	Appreciation of differing aims of business in different sectors (public, private and voluntary)	Identification of competing aims of stakeholders
Keeping owners satisfied		
Success for business compared with charity		

Area of Study 3: What resources do businesses use?

Foundation Level	General Level	Credit Level
3.1 Why do businesses locate where they do?		
Where businesses locate Where the money comes from – owner(s), borrowing	Sources of finance Factors influencing location – market, resources, infrastructure	Types of government assistance Importance of European Union Globalisation
3.2 How do people contribute to business?		
Why people work Choosing the right person for the job Job training Working hours Types of worker	Job/person specification	Selection and recruitment (internal and external) The role of appraisal Inter-relationship between employees and employers Changing patterns of employment
3.3 How do businesses use information?		
What information is and where it comes from Using computers to generate information – spreadsheets, databases, desktop publishing, word processing, networks, etc. Importance of good communications	Internal and external sources of information Using computers to generate information and make decisions	Evaluation of information Using information to monitor and control business
3.4 How do businesses operate?		
How businesses make products or provide services (input, process, output) How do products get to consumers?	Job, batch and flow processes People v. machines Distribution options	Stock control Quality assurance Customer service
3.5 What are the challenges facing businesses?		
Competition from home and abroad	Limited availability of resources and funding (external) Internal and external pressures	Appreciation of the impact on business of current political, legislative, social and environmental issues

Appendix

Area of Study 4: How are businesses managed?

Foundation Level	General Level	Credit Level
4.1 What are the key decisions that businesses make?		
What to produce	Market research	Inter-relationship between components of marketing mix
What to charge	Relationship between price and sales	
Who to employ		Combination of factors of production
Where to produce	People v. machines	
	Whether to grow	
4.2 What influences the decisions?		
Owner needs	The legal environment	The economic environment
Customer needs	The social environment	The political environment
Competition		
4.3 What aids decision making?		
How information helps decision making	Range of information used for decision making	Complex decision-making model
Types of information		
Decision-making model		
4.4 How are decisions made?		
Consensual v. authoritarian	Impact of management style on motivation and morale	Characteristics of effective management
4.5 How do businesses communicate?		
Purpose of communication	Formal/informal/internal/external	Comparison and evaluation of effectiveness of different communications
Process/methods of communication	Select and use appropriate IT	
Using IT to communicate	Select appropriate communication methods	Comparison and evaluation of ICT communications